The Dove
in
the Stone

Cover photo by Robert Glaze
of Artstreet

The Dove
in
the Stone

Finding the Sacred in the Commonplace

Alice O. Howell

*This publication made possible with
the assistance of the Kern Foundation*

The Theosophical Publishing House
Wheaton, Ill. U.S.A.
Madras, India/London, England

The Theosophical Publishing House
306 West Geneva Road
Wheaton, IL 60187
A publication of the Theosophical Publishing House, a depart-
ment of the Theosophical Society in America.

Library of Congress Cataloging in Publication Data

Howell, Alice O., 1922-
    The dove in the stone.
    (A Quest book)
    Bibliography: p.
    1. Iona (Scotland)--Miscellanea.   2. Howell,
Alice O., 1922-   I. Title.
BF1999.H77   1988   291.3'5'0941423   88-40181
ISBN 0-8356-0639-2 (pbk.)

Printed in the United States of America

For the "you" in this work
WALTER A. ANDERSEN
beloved husband, friend, teacher

When the last question
is asked
the answer will be molten gold—
love will have minted
more than life could hold.

A.O.

Table of Contents

foreword

Christopher Bamford

There is a path of love and knowledge to which the West is heir. Once on this path, the pilgrim is no longer alone, but in a visionary company of "friends of God." This community of saints, encountered by a simple gesture of consciousness, lies outside time and place in the soul's sacred and magic realm: the Imagination. Here the ancient sages of Egypt, Persia, Israel, and Greece are bound together in a kind of mystical chivalry or fellowship with Gnostic, Neoplatonic, and Christian fathers, as well as with the poets, saints, alchemists, and philosophers of more recent times. This prophetic religion of Sophia, forever moved by love and beauty, is a living transmission and a perpetual renaissance; it has no formal church or earthly institution, but is revealed only in the hearts and minds of human beings. Of the spirit, it is present whenever two or three are gathered together in the service of the ensouling of the world— of the return of the soul to God by way of the soul's return to her true self.

On the plane of history and geography, we find traces of such activity wherever truly dedicated souls arise. When they do, the earth is consecrated by their presence; places are made sacred and bear spiritual fruit. Grace descends gently there; it is in the very atmosphere, invisibly fertilizing those whose hearts are opened. Like the Scottish rain, misty at first, gradually and impercep-

tibly it soaks the pilgrim to the skin as he or she walks
in its nimbus as in a dream, drawn on by its balmy perfume. Iona is such an ensouled place. Columba and his
saints, who knew the wisdom of God in creation and
worshipped it continuously, have made it so. Iona's
power is such that it instructs all who walk there in the
arts of ensoulment. It is a place of soul and of imagination, sacrament and the feminine. No wonder, then, that
Alice O. Howell set her book on that little island in the
West. But Iona can be any place where the heart is open.
For when the heart is open, we enter the realm of the
imagination, that active mirror in which spirit takes
form in images and matter is immateralized. Here spiritual and human love become one in the divine play that
weaves the stars and holds the earth, the sky, humanity, and the divine in a single creative gesture of knowing. This is the soul realm, which we have lost.

The Dove in the Stone begins to return us to this realm
of meaning. By doing so it takes its place in an honorable
countertradition that has upheld the standard of the soul
(the feminine and the imagination) throughout the dark
night of the past millennium. We may call this the Trou-
badour lineage. The poet Rilke points to this in his novel
The Notebooks of Malte Laurids Brigge when he claims
that it is women who have been the great teachers of
love and that men have but haltingly repeated what
women have taught them.

Alice knows this great truth in her bones: she is a
woman, she has been there. But beyond this life knowledge, she knows by heart the mystical, theological
teaching embodied in it. She knows that this feminine
aspect of wisdom, which is love, is Holy Sophia. In the

Valentinian myth of the soul, Sophia is the youngest of the divine syzygies, or pairs, who conceives an impossible passion to know her father directly and alone. For this indiscretion, she falls from the purest spirituality into the utter sensuality and darkness of ignorance where, out of her own fallen psychical substance (her cupidity, travail, and agony), matter is solidified into terrestrial reality. Here, amid the phantasms of her own creation, as *Sophia Prunikos* (Sophia the Whore, in contrast to Celestial Sophia), she wanders grief-stricken, fearful, and abandoned, until the Logos descends to rescue her.

In this sense, Sophia, the divine feminine, is no other than the human soul herself in her pain and suffering. United with the Logos, her celestial self, Sophia, the mother of all spiritual creation, leads her children back into fellowship with the divine. As the unfallen and the fallen soul, Sophia represents the possibility of divine love—the possibility all creatures have of emptying themselves of egotism so that love might enter in. In Christian theology this power is the wholeness and integrity—the beauty—of creation itself. By this beauty, and the love it inspires, creation is able to plunge into the mind and heart of God. Sophia, the soul, is thus "withness" with God. She is both what is divine in creation and what is created in the divine. She is the great mediator between the uncreated and the created, the guardian angel, the ideal form of world, by whom God thinks all things and through whom he is enabled to become all in all.

For Rilke, this feminine element—which is love, and is the very life of humanity—is the ground of wisdom, of imagination. Therefore, at the center of his book, he places a description of those medieval tapestries that depict this path in images of a woman and a unicorn. Here the woman feeds a falcon; now she weaves a garland. Here she sits beside her tent, while above it is emblazoned: *Á mon seul désir* (To my only desire). Now, with one hand, she grasps the unicorn's horn. Her other arm inclines toward it. The unicorn leaps toward her, into her lap. In her hand she has a mirror: *she is showing the unicorn its image in the mirror.*

This is exactly what Alice O. Howell does in her book. *The Dove in the Stone* is written from, by, and for the soul. And the soul, the world's beauty—Sophia—is the only bond between spirit and matter. Only soul, another word for which is imagination, can reveal the spirit's presence. Only the Sophianic soul, the feminine aspect of wisdom, can hold up the mirror and be the spirit's place.

Acknowledgments

I would like to extend my thanks for the loving encouragement and help received not only from my husband Walter Andersen, but from Christopher Bamford and Tadea Dufault, and Rod and Sue Welles, fellow travelers to Iona; to Edith Wallace and Maggie Smith, blessed catalysts in my life; to Nicky Hearon and Elizabeth W. Ferry for assistance in research; to Helen Pellathy, Jean MacIntyre, Mary Leonard, Brian and Jeralyn Scott-McCarthy, and Roger Woolger for their contributions; and, especially to Shirley Nicholson, editor exemplary. And, of course, to the Fairy Godmother!

I would like to thank the following for allowing me to print their material:

Edmund Keeley and Philip Sherrard, trans. *C.P. Cavafy: Collected Poems.* Ed. by George Savadis. Trans. copyright ©1975 by E. Keeley and P. Sherrard. "Ithaka" reprinted with permission of Princeton University.

Mircea Eliade, *A History of Religious Ideas*, vol. II, p. 416, the paragraph on Demeter. Willard R. Trask, trans. ©1982 by Mircea Eliade. Reprinted with permission of The University of Chicago Press.

Douglas Hyde, trans. "The Mystery," from *1000 Years of Irish Poetry*, ed. by Kathleen Hoagland, 1962. Reprinted with the permission of Grosset & Dunlap.

"There is a tree that grows in me" from *Something's Sleeping in the Hall* by Karla Kuskin. Copyright ©1985 by Karla Kuskin. Reprinted by permission of Harper & Row, Publishers, Inc.

Kook, Rav Abraham, "A Thirst for the Living God," Burt Jacobson, trans. *Gnosis 3: A Journal of the Western Inner Traditions*. Fall/Winter 1986-87. San Francisco: Lumen Foundations. Reprinted by permission.

R.F.C. Hull, trans. *The Collected Works of C.G. Jung*. Bollingen Series, 20 vols. 1957-79. Princeton: Princeton University Press. Short excerpts.

These philosophers suspected that a "spirit" was imprisoned there in the vessel of matter; a "white dove" comparable to the Nous in the krater of Hermes of which it is said: "Plunge into this krater, if thou canst, by recognizing to what end thou wast created, and by believing that thou wilt rise up to Him, who sent the krater down to earth."

Corpus Hermeticum IV, 4

For the Celts the mundane was the edge of glory.

Esther de Waal

I

The Edge of Glory

It is a long way to Iona. Even today it will take the modern pilgrim hours by boat, by bus or car, and then again by boat to reach this tiny, precious island in the Hebrides—the Isle of Iona. This was the eleventh time I was coming home to it, and no longer alone! I looked over at you fondly—a big burly polar bear of a man, over seventy, with white hair, rosy face, and laughter crinkles around smiling eyes. Camera at the ready, you were trying to catch a gull soaring higher and higher above you without a single flap of wing.

We had been married four years now, and this was your first trip to Scotland. We looked out together at the fair clean sea, rimmed as it was with beauty, tier upon tier of distant mountains fading back from blue-green, to blue, to violet, to pearl. Here, as the song goes, "sleeps the noon in the deep blue sky." I hugged the rail with the secret joy of being able to share it with you.

Walter on the boat at Mull

The boat from Oban, the port in the northwest of Scotland, was not crowded, since it was fall, and the sail over to Mull continued, a freshness of sun and wind, a clearing of the soul.

Leaning against the railing, I was reminded again of the Buddhist meditation on the Land of Pure Bliss and its Celtic equivalent, the Land of Heart's Desire, the *Tir nan Og*, the Happy Isles, the archetypal Land of Eternal Youth. This, in turn, took me back to my childhood, for here surely my story begins as it does for us all.

When I was little, almost five years old, my life changed drastically. I sailed from New York with my parents on a huge liner to Europe. From then on for many years I learned a lot about waiting and separation. I sat on a great number of trunks and suitcases and hat boxes in cavernous, cold and grey railway stations, waiting for my parents to buy tickets in London or Istanbul, in Lausanne or Rome or other cities. It could be late at night or very early in the morning, and I would sit there waiting, trying to read the peeling steamship and hotel labels and hugging my stuffed terrier with the fraying ears.

These stations were iron and glass caves, under the domes of which blue-smocked porters would push and pull bales and luggage on wagons, shouting strange imprecations to each other in incomprehensible languages. The air was always dim and filled with the dust and incense of coal. It felt like living in a dirty glass. People looked more like wraiths, their voices losing resonance in a mysterious way. A sepulchral fear would come over me. Off again, from the unknown to the unknown.

Sometimes, my father would disappear, sometimes my mother, and sometimes both, leaving me to board the Orient Express with the nurse or governess of the period. We lived and often slept on trains.

By the time I was twelve, my father's work had led us to over thirty-six countries, and I had also learned a great deal about exile. Painful partings from parents, from childhood friends, and from places cherished. But hidden in the pain was also a gift, one "invented" by my mother, for on realizing my growing distress and anxiety, she hit upon the idea of an imaginary land where every night we might all meet together, no matter how distant we were from one another. Needless to say, as a child alone in hotels without radio or television in those days, the charm and overwhelming power of this suggestion was immediately apparent.

It would be thirty years before I would hear of the Buddhist meditation on the Land of Pure Bliss and even longer before I would grasp what Carl Gustav Jung meant when he spoke of archetypes as primordial images in the collective unconscious. But I do know it comes instinctively and naturally to a child to be in touch with this numinosity. In no time at all, the imaginary land was patently "real" to me, and populated with archetypal characters, magical animals, and all the phantasmagoria that my unconscious, and that of my parents, allowed to emerge, nurtured surely by Bible readings, fairy tales and myths as they came my way.

I continued to reflect on this, as the boat headed up the bay towards Mull, passing the stolid square tower of Duart, the old castle seat of the Clan Maclean. There had been two surprising elements in the emergence of this inner landscape. The first was that, even though I shared the names and characters with my mother and even occasionally with my father, when I climbed into bed and closed my eyes and boarded the little train which would carry me there, when I got to Beejumstan itself, I never *did* meet my parents there, nor did I even miss them. I had found my archetypal mentors, a Wise Old Man called Gezeebius and a Fairy Godmother called Mercy Muchmore.

Now that I am entering what my children describe as the "youth of my old age," I have reason, good reason, to reexamine this subliminal land and its folk, and to see that all along they have been hidden within the outer reality of my life. I am not for a second suggesting that I had access as a child to *the* Pure Land. I am only saying that I have not forgotten or denied the empirical experience that I had of one reality hidden within another, which added a dimension of comfort and delight to my life and was, whenever I honored it, a source of symbolic wisdom. Its very spontaneous existence strikes me as a possible parallel in children to what perhaps was experienced and shared by early or primitive man in centuries past or Aborigines in present times, and which in a humble way is where we start our quest for the archetypal Kingdom of Heaven. That the wee folk dwelt in our land and angels and archangels or devas or houris dwell on the higher levels, seemed natural to me then and even now. It's the process of finding, losing, yearning and rediscovering such an alternate reality that we all share, in one way or another, that lies at the bottom of our quest. This, too, is the basis of our

sense of being exiled in this life, more often than not,
whenever the magic fails and meaning is lost. We are
all of us, whether we are conscious of it or not, on a
journey looking for what to *us* would be sacred.

As the Caledonia moved out again into open waters,
we crossed to the starboard side. The colors now reminded me of Greece, and this in turn of C. V. Cavafy's
beautiful poem that expresses much the same idea as the
one motivating this book.

ITHAKA

As you set out for Ithaka
hope your road is a long one,
full of adventure, full of discovery.
Laistrygonians, Cyclops,
angry Poseidon—don't be afraid of them:
you'll never find things like that on your way
as long as you keep your thoughts raised high,
as long as a rare excitement
stirs your spirit and your body.
Laistrygonians, Cyclops,
wild Poseidon—you won't encounter them
unless you bring them along inside your soul,
unless your soul sets them up in front of you.

Hope your road is a long one.
May there be many summer mornings when,
with what pleasure, what joy,
you enter harbors you're seeing for the first time;
may you stop at Phoenician trading stations
to buy fine things,
mother of pearl and coral, amber and ebony,
sensual perfume of every kind—
as many sensual perfumes as you can;
and may you visit many Egyptian cities
to learn and go on learning from their scholars.

Keep Ithaka always in your mind.
Arriving there is what you're destined for.
But don't hurry the journey at all.
Better if it lasts for years,
so you're old by the time you reach the island,
wealthy with all you've gained on the way,
not expecting Ithaka to make you rich.
Ithaka gave you the marvelous journey.
Without her you wouldn't have set out.
She has nothing left to give you now.

And if you find her poor, Ithaka won't have fooled you.
Wise as you will have become, so full of experience,
you'll have understood by then what these Ithakas mean.
                                                    C. V. Cavafy

The second surprising element in my childhood's experience is more personal. It had to do with the actual landscape of my Pure Land. Its topography was of such supernal beauty that despite all my travels, I had never seen it. It could not exist. Then one day, when I was in my mid-forties and living on Long Island, I was looking through a book of pictures—and there it was! An area which, surprisingly enough, I had never been to: the islands off the northwest coast of Scotland, the Inner and Outer Hebrides.

At that time there was no chance of finding out, one way or another, whether they truly were identical. I put the book back on the shelf in the library and told myself I would only be disappointed anyway. I was married to my first husband then, with four young children, very little money, and it was all nonsense anyway.

Then, out of nowhere, a few weeks later, a lady appeared on our doorstep. Her name was Margaret

Stewart, and she had come to see my husband's artwork. As she passed by the wall of books I had, she asked me if I happened to know anything about St. Martin's Cross on Iona, or if I could find out something about it. She needed a picture of it. Immediately I began a systematic search, going from book to book. I did not find a picture, but I began to read more and more bits about Iona, St. Columba, and the Hebrides. Deep bells were ringing in me; I was excited, and silently I made a vow to get to Iona somehow, someday.

A month later, a dear friend of mine, a woman my mother's age, died, leaving me a sum of money, much to my astonishment. I decided to go to the British Isles with my youngest daughter (the only one young enough for half-fare) and a friend of hers as soon as school ended. I had plans to take students abroad in future summers and saw this as a pilot trip.

So off we went. We began the trip in England but soon headed north towards Scotland. I began to be fearful, very fearful of disappointment. It could not possibly be as beautiful as the land of my dreaming. That would be like finding heaven on earth.

But it was. Indeed, that is where and when and how I first experienced the fact that heaven (as well as hell) can be on earth. It all depends on one's consciousness. Somehow, when I stepped onto Iona the first time, the inner landscape suffused the outer, or the outer embodied the inner, and as I stood actually looking up at that great carved stone Celtic cross, some inner conviction took hold: there is an inner beauty in each of us hungering to be matched in outer experience. When this happens in truth, some great affirmation leaps up within us and for a moment out of time, we move from hope and belief to certainty.

I went into the abbey for the first time and sat on one of the hard wooden chairs. I felt the presence of the old stones around me, and I tried to sort out the illogical depth of my feelings. What was it here? The girls explored the cloisters while I prayed as I had never prayed before. Prayed that I might return, that I might learn more of what I was experiencing so directly. Finally I got up and walked around the church itself. I found a niche below a small stained glass window of St. Columba. A vase of wildflowers stood lit by a rare shaft of sunlight. In front of it rested a black pyramidal stone. It said: Take me with you. You will not be sorry. I am yours.

I took the stone. It was my stone. Later, and in subsequent visits, I discovered stones hidden all about the abbey like Easter eggs. There are probably stones of Iona all over the world. There is one, I know, embedded in the altar of the Church of St. Andrew in Sewanee, Tennessee; there are many at Chinook on Whidbey Island across from Seattle, and since then I have carried many others home for friends over the years. Everybody seems impelled to take these mute missionaries with them. Stones of Iona.

Such were my thoughts as the boat eased up to the jetty at Craignure, and you, my dear one, and I made our descent into its clanging bowels to find our car. There were the diesel fumes into which rose the sound

Tadea Dufault

St. Martin's cross

of pleasant voices, all with a Gaelic lilt: men, women, children, dogs and, added to the friendly confusion, the anxious mooing of cows and calves. In another pen a flock of black-faced sheep baaed their parts into the chorus.

We still had Mull to cross before sunset, where we would leave the car and catch the last ferry over to the island. We drove off the boat, and with a clank and a thud were on the solid ground of our first Hebridean island. We turned left at the dock and headed through the fir trees to the silent silver road that leads through the majesty of Mull. There the clouds were casting the swiftly sailing darkness of their shadows in huge indigo sweeps across the moors. All the earth here seems always alive with a shimmering presence. It conjured up the words from the song "The Road to the Isles": "O the far Cuillins are putting love on me as step I with my cromag to the isles." You could feel the enfolding quality of these mountains of Mull. Traditionally, many of the mountains in the Highlands were called the paps or breasts of the Celtic goddess who lies stretched out and dreaming in the undulating earth. It could be a fair or a "terrible beauty" according to her weather mood. Our eyes, indeed, filled with awe. Life here is "to be sung with ecstatic serenity," as my Celtic song book suggests.

Before long, we had made the traverse, left the car at Fionnphort, and boarded the little ferry to the Sacred Isle.

Next morning, I continued my thoughts. Since that first trip I had returned to Iona, by hook and with crook, ten more times over the years. I am writing these words on Iona now, and if I stretch a little I can see Mull dreaming pink in the distance with huge clouds lowering, grey and silver, scudding over Ben More. The sound is a blue-lilac calm below, and to the left I can just see the great silent uplifted arms of St. Martin's cross. What is it calling me back, what is it needs to be shared?

Suddenly I know. I have come back first of all to ask about stones.

Cleave a piece of wood, I am there;
lift up the stone and you will find me there.
                    The Gospel according to Thomas

CONTEMPLATION OF ONE STONE

There are three stones:

the one I see
the one imaged and now part of me
and the one that is there—

One more
would make four.
Where is the stone I saw?

No matter what I do
the stone and I make two.

Wait, no!

One

Now I am rock and everywhere.
                    A.O.

The dove soaring above the cere-
mony and suffusing it with heavenly
light symbolizes the "royal art"
which the Rosarium Philosophorum
terms a gift of the Holy Ghost.
        Notes on an alchemical treatise

Let the soul of man take the whole
universe for its body.
                    Simone Weil

II

Stones

"Come with me," I invited. I could hardly wait to share Iona with you. So you went to put on your white fisherman's sweater which just matched your hair, and to get your walking shoes on. Finally, hand in hand, we set off together.

We walked north past the abbey, then headed due west over the island, no doubt following the tracks of St. Columba and his monks. "Who was St. Columba?" you asked. I told you that he was the Ramakrishna of his time: he bridged two religious views and was the spiritual father and grandfather to disciples who were, through their inner incandescence, to spread a new approach to God over Europe—for Columba's monks, a Celtic rather than a Roman way. A sixth-century Irish prince, he was tutored by Druids before becoming a wise, strong and gentle Christian. Unlike the Roman patriarchs, he sought not to destroy the old views but to enhance them and bring them to flower. For the Celtic Christians this meant not destroying the old pagan holy sites, but building upon them. At Cashel in Ireland, for example, there was a rock on which the Irish had

crowned their kings. Here the Celtic Christians set up
a statue of Christ, their King of kings. For them, unlike
the Romans, continuing the Celtic tradition meant loving and honoring nature and always finding holiness
within it. By some strange synchronicity, St. Columba,
whose name in Latin means *dove*, arrived on Iona
(which is the Hebrew word for *dove*) with twelve disciples on the Eve of Pentecost, May 12, 563—the day of
the ascent of the Holy Spirit in the Christian calendar,
also symbolized by a dove.

We crossed *Liana nan Curracag*, Gaelic for the
Meadow of the Lapwings, buffeted, as ever, by the fresh
heather-scented wind. Within minutes we were alone
under a vast sky with nothing about but rocks and more
rocks, rising and falling around us, all of them tucked
in and about with a rough blanket of turf, which was
often wet and squelchy under our feet. By squeezing
through the wire sheep fences, we continued past the
Hill of the Brownie to the beaches facing *Camus Cul
an Taibh*, the Bay at the Back of the Ocean. I wanted
to get back, not to the cool white sands, but to the beach
of the stones.

Now we could sit among them. They have to be the
most beautiful rounded, smooth, subtly colored stones
in the world. They are about the size of large rolls of
bread. Despite the breeze, the sea was calm here this
day, an eerie sheening sheet of crystal light extending
all the way to the horizon and broken only by dark islets
in the distance. But the edge of it was close to us, murmuring and sucking at these old and patient stones.
Watered rock, rocked by water. Wherever the water wet
them the stones flashed into glistening jewels: polished

Stones east of the abbey

Camus Cul an Taibn

quartz, feldspar, hornblende, even marble. The ones,
like us, above the tide awaited their turn. On Iona you
can almost hear them speak. But here one must learn
to hear the voice of silence.

We know now that this island is made up of the most
ancient rock on earth. Geologically speaking, Iona is
quite different even from its closest neighbor, the Isle
of Mull, which is only a mile and a half away. Perhaps
it is left over from some antediluvian age. In any case,
to sit here and listen is to go back into one's own bones,
to know that they share something in common with the
stardust of origin and with the secrets of titans and of
stone gods and god stones.

You picked up one at random. It was grey and striated
with whirling loops of darker and lighter grey, with
white spots at either end. "It looks like a galaxy," you
remarked, "like a universe." And so it did.

The connections between stones and humankind are
indeed many. Mysteriously, during the Stone Age, our
forebears set up stone circles, gilgals, dolmens, and
menhirs as sacred markers, as places for ritual and sacrifice. These sites are not only evident in Britain, but
are to be found in Europe, on Malta, in Israel, India,
and perhaps even in North America. Today such places
are being studied scientifically in an attempt to decipher
the sophisticated astronomical knowledge that these ancient people had.

The Old Testament provides many references to the
magical properties of stones, from Jacob's Pillow to the
breastplate of twelve gems worn by Hebrew priests; from

the altars of the Canaanites (in the Age of Taurus) to
that of the Israelites which was set up with ram's horns
at its four corners (in the Age of Aries). After Jacob slept
on his stone and dreamt of the ladder with angels as-
cending and descending, he took the stone and set it up
for a pillar, and poured oil upon it and called it Beth-
El—The House of God. I wonder whether all stones are
not houses of God? In the Middle Ages quite a few men
and women, the Beguines and the Beghards, went to
their death in flames as heretics for suggesting such a
thing. Hopefully, we are getting humbler and wiser.

Greek mythology tells of the Great Flood sent by Zeus
to punish mankind. Only Deucalion and Pyrrha sur-
vived. When they consulted the oracle, they heard a
message: "Throw the bones of your mother over your
shoulder." This they finally interpreted as meaning to
throw stones over their shoulders, since rocks are the
bones of the Great Mother Earth. So they did, and the
stones Deucalion threw became men, and the stones Pyrrha threw became women. This is surely a reminder to
us that our bodystuff is of the mineral kingdom, something we should not forget. I thought of the great Sufi
Rumi's poem:

> *I died from mineral, and plant became*
> *Died from the plant and took a sentient frame;*
> *Died from the beast, and donned a human dress;*
> *When by dying did I e'er grow less:*
> *Another time from manhood I must die*
> *To soar with angel-pinions through the sky.*
> *'Midst Angels also I must lose my place,*
> *Since "Everything shall perish save His Face."*
> *Let me be Naught! The harp-strings tell me plain*
> *That unto Him do we return again!*
> > *The Mathnawi*

As an astrologer, I found myself musing about how strange it was that just as Neptune recently entered Saturn's sign of Capricorn, so many people have become preoccupied by crystals and their powers. Not just "New Age" people, but the entire computer industry and users of silicon microchips. The slowly changing attitude towards our planet is being brought about by a great generation of people born with Neptune in Virgo, an earth sign. As Neptune trines this, a shift, like a tide, may come to save her before it is too late.

For thousands of years we have looked skyward to heaven searching for the divine, and have spurned our own planet Earth. We have seen it, in fact, as a place of temptation and tribulation, a place to which Adam and Eve "fell" from Eden only to labor by the sweat of their brows for the rest of their days. We still pray for our children at baptism, and again in the confirmation service, that they may renounce the "pomps and vanities of this wicked world." As Matthew Fox has pointed out, this is the view of "Fall and Redemption" theology. From a Jungian perspective, it is the logical conclusion for us who are identified with the ego to project a transcendent God "out there." The profound myth of Adam and Eve prefigures the necessary fall and redemption of that ego before we are ready to reach for the inner Self, or God immanent "within" us. It is a tremendous shift of viewpoint!

Slowly, slowly, however, collectively we are changing, and the new theology speaks of a "creation-centered spirituality." For many of us this means a return of the goddess—or the feminine aspect of the Godhead— fostering a love and appreciation of our planet and its creatures, and a new ecology. If any stone is the House of God, by extension, then Earth itself is mother to meaning, to consciousness itself. It makes me think of Shakespeare's words:

> *Sweet are the uses of adversity,*
> *Which, like the toad, ugly and venomous,*
> *Wears yet a precious jewel in his head,*
> *And this our life, exempt from public haunt,*
> *Finds tongues in trees, books in the running brooks,*
> *Sermons in stones, and good in everything.*
> > *As You Like It, Act II,*
> > *Scene i, lines 12-17*

There is a legend on Iona, perpetuated in the name of a place called The Glen of the Temple, that even before the arrival of Columba, Iona was a sacred isle, a place with a circle of standing stones, a place, eventually, where kings were buried and carried along The Road of the Dead. It has been proposed that some of these great stones were carved into the high Celtic crosses. There are suggestions that Columba, too, had a stone pillow. Whether this stone is literally the one is not so important, it is the tradition that counts. The Stone of Destiny, the Coronation Stone at Westminster, is believed to have come from Iona.

And what can we make of Theseus, Arthur, and Sigmund, all heroes in comparable Greek, Celtic, and Teutonic mythologies, proving their strength by pulling the magic sword from stones or trees? These images are all hints emerging from the collective unconscious and pointing to the star in the stone, the hidden energy and wisdom concealed in what was once despised "matter." Over and over again, we have brushed aside these tales as fanciful, not seeing the hidden process. Over and over, we are robbed by the literalism which paralyzes our symbolic thinking and living, as surely as Medusa paralyzed her victims, turning them into stones! When Perseus used the "reflection" of his shield to kill her, he decapitated her and released the lovely winged Pegasus trapped inside. Surely there is a Pegasus hidden at the heart of every literalism within us waiting for release.

Then there is the motif of the *petra genetrix*, the birth-giving stone. Mithra, the bullslayer with the Phrygian cap, was born of a rock on December 25. He was the savior in Mithraism, a religion which rivaled Christianity in the first three centuries A.D. Now, as Jung has pointed out, a myth is not necessarily true from a literal point of view, but from a psychic perspective. "A myth," he said, "is always true of the psyche."

So, if we probe the connection of Christmas to the birth of Mithra and to the Roman Saturnalian festivals that it replaced, we find the motif of the return of the light of the Sun at the darkest time of the year. This is a physical fact, but on another level it speaks to the mystery of the rebirth of the inner light within us. The mystery of incarnation works two ways: spirit takes on form, and form is hidden spirit. Light answers to light. The stones leap godward. We know now that the atoms they are made of are swirling microcosms of energy, of life. So as you sat there holding the "stone galaxy" in your hand on that beach, it was alive—a microcosmic house of energy we can call divine, a House of God. It tells us that life really *matters*, since matter has life. (In Latin, by the way, the word matter is cognate to *mother*, *mater*.)

The holiest shrine of all for Moslems is the Ka'bah in Mecca. In it is a small black stone, probably a meteorite. In Jerusalem at the Dome of the Rock is an immense rock which is reputed to be the site where Abraham almost sacrificed Isaac. It became the site of Solomon's Temple, and the place from which Muhammad ascended on his steed for "The Ride into the Mystical Night." Below, just yards away, is the Wailing Wall, where I myself and many others have felt a swaying of the stones, so saturated are they with history and passion. In every sense, certain stones and stone cathedrals, monuments and markers would seem to have been the receivers of human attention and devotion. To believe that they hold special energy or "vibrations" has been considered idolatry and superstition, pagan magic, heresy. And yet for the human psyche at some level it remains profoundly meaningful. Why?

Perhaps the answer to this lies in the "Stone of Stones": the Philosopher's Stone. To find the *lapis philosophorum, the calculus alba,* the "stone of a thousand names" was the great goal of the medieval alchemists. By its touch, the alchemist would be able to transform lead into gold, though the alchemists themselves claimed the result to be *non aurum vulgum,* or not an ordinary metallic gold. What did they mean? It was this process that fascinated Jung so much, and since then Edward F. Edinger, Nathan Schwartz-Salant and others, who have found in the complex language of alchemy a parallel to the psychological processes of growth appearing in the dreams and the active imaginations of their patients. It seems to represent the union of opposites—the mystical marriage within the psyche of God Within, as Self, with the human center of personality and consciousness, the Ego.

Out of this union may spring that reborn child in us which can see the *unus mundus*, "the one world," which is "that heaven spread upon earth" men do not see.

For me, as we sat in the cooling luminous air of Iona, it seemed as if the struggle to find the Philosopher's Stone might end if one ceased to struggle so hard. Perhaps it was a matter of seeing that every stone could be a Philosopher's Stone if you knew the "philosopher" hiding within it. (In Greek, the word *philosopher* means a *lover of Wisdom*, a big clue!) Now, if I were to ask you to close your eyes and picture a philosopher, what would you see?

Invariably almost all of us picture an older man, with or without a beard, seriously disposed, dignified and wise. Yet, here on this holy island of doves may lie a secret the world is hungering for: maybe the philosophic archetype we are seeking is not an old wise man. It could be a playful woman of delights, whose name is Holy Wisdom, Hagia Sophia! According to prophecy, her time has come. If this is a New Age, then this is the Age of the Holy Spirit according to Joachim of Floris, a medieval monk. He likened the age of the Old Testament to the Age of the Father, which was Law; and the age of the New Testament to the Age of the Son, which was the Gospel; the Age of the Holy Ghost, to this day symbolized by the dove, was yet to come. I believe from all the indications that this is our own Age of Aquarius.

One word of caution—one that I learned both from my teacher, M, with whom I studied in New York, and from Jung. We are not speaking literally here, we are speaking symbolically. What we are looking for on earth

and in earth and in our lives is the *process* that can unlock for us the mystery of meaningfulness in our daily
lives. It has been the best-kept secret down through the
ages because it is so simple. Truly, the last place it would
ever occur to most of us to find the sacred would be in
the commonplace of our everyday lives and all about
us in nature and in simple things.

Apparently, we need to distinguish between pantheism and panentheism. Pantheism for Christian theologians has always been a heresy, the idea that everything
and everyone is God. The argument goes even today and
is used against "New Age" thinking: "If any man is God,
then any act is potentially a sacrament, any idea potentially sacred." This is dangerous to society, I quite agree.
Ideas and acts proceeding from the ego level alone are
not what is meant! The theological and psychological
thrust of the next two millennia are to be spent in acquir-
ing and surrendering the ego in all humility to that Light
within, by whatever name you call it, that is One with
God. As we grow to this level, we will begin to see things
and each other quite differently. Panentheism would say
that God is both immanent and transcendent, and that
spirit is in all things. This seems to be less of a threat
to orthodox hieratic thinking. Yet, "Lift a stone," said
Christ, "and I am there." Or as Peter puts it in his First
Epistle: "So come to him, our living Stone—the stone
rejected by men but choice and precious in the sight of
God. Come and let yourselves be built, as living stones,
into a spiritual temple."

We sat at the beach a while longer listing a few of
the names Sophia goes by. It is a lovely litany. Yes, she

is Judaic, she is Christian, she is Buddhist, she is Moslem, she was and is and will be everywhere that anything is manifest in form.

I asked her, as I held the stone in my hand, if she wanted me to write a scholarly and well-researched book about her, something to occupy me for the rest of my life. I think I heard a smile. "Mercy, no! find me in life, in art and music and poetry which touch you; find me in nature, in its mathematics, and in the geometry of being; find me in images, in laughter, and the heart's wisdom. Find me in your soul! Come with me, and I will teach you to look with a loving eye."

Looking at you made that an easy lesson, and on our way back across the island a rare, lonely beauty stretched everywhere. Crossing a bog, you stepped into wet earth up to your knee and you almost lost your shoe. You would have to buy a stout pair of Wellingtons, those rubber boots my mother insisted on calling Waterloos! We laughed our way back to the coffee shop run by the Iona Community, and there enjoyed a hot cup of tea and currant-filled scones. It had been a fine time.

The most touching episode of...Deme-
ter took place at the beginning of
February 1940, and it was recounted
and commented on at length in the
Athenian press. At one of the bus stops
between Athens and Corinth there
came on board an old woman, "thin
and dried up but with very big and
keen eyes." Since she had no money to
pay her fare, the driver made her leave
the bus at the next stop—which was
precisely, Eleusis. But the driver could
not get the motor started again; finally
the passengers decided to chip in and
pay the old woman's fare. She got back
on board, and this time the bus set off.
Then the old woman said to them:
"You ought to have done it sooner, but
you are egotists; and since I am among
you, I will tell you something else: you
will be punished for the way you live,
you will be deprived even of plants and
water!" "She had not finished threaten-
ing them," the author of the article
published in Hestia goes on, "before she
vanished....No one had seen her get
out. Then the passengers looked at one
another, and they examined the ticket
stubs again to make sure that a ticket
had indeed been issued."
                              Mircea Eliade

Symbols themselves are theophanies of the absolute in the
relative.

The central postulate of the Way is that there is a hidden
meaning in all things. Every thing has an outer as well as
inner meaning. Every external form is complemented by
an inner reality which is its hidden eternal essence.
                    Nader Ardalan and Laleh Bhaktiar

III

The Chi-ops Connection

After a warm bath and a good supper at the hotel, we went into a corner of the lounge for a postprandial coffee. Out the window we could see the last pink and lavender clouds behind the Ross of Mull. The Sound of Iona was pure silver, and that heavenly shimmering light that is the gift of the north was holding the strong tolling of the abbey bell and spreading the clang of it over the island to summon the Community to evening worship. This night we chose to stay where we were.

"What was the story you hinted at about your own stone of Iona?" you asked. Still considering ourselves "newlyweds," we had so many stories of our former lives to share. In fact, we never seem to run out of them.

"Well," I answered, "it is a strange one, to be sure, and I have no explanation for it. All I can say is that it happened."

Several years ago I gave a week-long workshop at Wainwright House in Rye, New York, on "Living the Symbolic Life." At the end of it, one of the participants

came up to me and asked me if I would mind her pro-
posing me for the faculty of a pilgrimage tour of the
Mediterranean called CHI-OPS. The tour was being or-
ganized in California. My chances of being included
seemed out of the question, but to humor her I agreed.
The next day she showed me a handwritten letter, which
she duly mailed. I forgot about it.

Several weeks later I received a letter inviting me to
go on the trip as a participant, to which I wrote back
a humorous and wistful letter: If only! Next, I got a
phone call from the leader, Maggie Smith, and we had
a wonderful conversation. Brugh Joy, the physician, and
Rosalyn Bruyere, the healing psychic, and Lawrence
Blair, the author of *Rhythms of Vision*, and Fritjof
Capra, the physicist, and James Fadiman, the transper-
sonal psychologist, were the faculty. I explained that it
was out of the question for me financially, but I enthusiastically agreed it was a great idea to go on such a
meaningful trip to the holy sites of antiquity bringing
a New Age perspective, a kind of joining of old and new.
Yes, it was true that I had traveled to almost all of those
places before, that I had taught ancient history and com-
parative religions for eighteen years and that I had a
strong belief in Jung's concept of the collective unconscious. My only potential contribution that I could think
of in such illustrious company would be an appreciative
rather than a scholarly commentary; this I had already
done for several years in the British Isles with students
of my own. I hung up the phone. Shortly thereafter came
another call. Would I join the faculty? Would I ever!

Within a matter of weeks I found myself joining 350
New Age pilgrims in Greece, and boarding a luxury liner
headed for Knossos (on Crete) and Egypt. My roommate

was a dear friend, Dr. Edith Wallace, who had studied with both Carl and Emma Jung and was a practising Jungian analyst in New York.

Our first experience was at Epidaurus, the great healing center of ancient Greece associated with Asclepius. This was of great interest to the many psychotherapists among us, since the Greeks had believed in patients going there specifically to undergo an incubation in the temple while praying for a dream which would then be interpreted. Here also was the Tholos of Polycleitus, the equivalent of a labyrinthian "snake pit" into the darkness of which a patient would be dropped and would have to feel his way out. The ensuing panic would be the equivalent of a rebirthing process, and some ventured that certain chemicals would be released in the brain under those circumstances that could cure depression as well as any shock treatment! Though the top of the Tholos was uncovered, it still gave me the shivers to look at it.

We visited the statues of Asclepius, the god of medicine, and Rosalyn Bruyere pointed out that he was always accompanied by a snake; the snake rising from the earth, sometimes wound about a staff to touch his finger and give him the feminine telluric energy which heals. This does not come down from on high, but up from below. Rosalyn, a remarkable young woman and a brilliant teacher, had us planting our feet on the good earth and feeling the strength rising into us, almost like sap up a tree. Again and again, this motif of the strength and goodness inherent in the upward movement of the feminine was repeated, and I could not help but think of Dante and Goethe and the many mystics who spoke of the upward-drawing powers of the feminine. Not, mind you, just of women by gender, but the entire process that is within both men and women—call it what you will—which can lead us back to God. As we know, she goes by many names.

Next we visited the immense open amphitheater and, linking hands, climbed and wound our way back and forth until we reached the top rows. I remember the beauty of the mottled stones, so perfectly arranged, and now covered here and there with mosses and little flowers in the cracks. At the top, with olive trees around and behind us, we all sat down and listened to the perfect acoustics demonstrated by the speakers far below us. Then we fell silent and meditated.

When we came down I was accosted by an astonished German family. "What is going on? Is this a religion?" No. "Then is this a society?" I tried to explain that until three days ago we had never met one another. They threw up their hands, dumbfounded. "These Americans! They never met each other and there they are all holding hands!" We continued to astonish, believe me! That was only the beginning.

As we sailed from Crete towards Port Said in Egypt, the group assembled on board for lectures and classes, interrupted by all the pleasures afforded tourists on a splendid cruise. But the evening before we were to land, Brugh Joy gave a preview of what we might expect at the Great Pyramid of Gizeh.

He himself had spent a night alone in the King's Chamber, which he described in his book *Joy's Way*. He told of the heat, the fetid air, and the dark and narrow passages, such as the one to the Queen's Chamber, too low to stand up in; the one up to the King's Chamber which is so narrow that as people climb up, they are pressing against those climbing down. The more he talked about it, the more uncomfortable I began to feel. That night, as I lay in my berth, I remembered that the Great Pyramid covers thirteen acres and has more than a million blocks of stone, each weighing over a ton. A claustrophobic sense of fear and potential failure settled on me. As you know, dear, I am not exactly young, nor could anyone describe me as skinny, and since I was struck by a car in Oban, I had a back that could go out without warning, for which I had Woodstock, my staff. What to do?

Well, I reasoned that the worst that could happen would be that I would die, and it would be an interesting place to do that. But I felt that I really should have a more positive approach. What could motivate me the most? Suddenly I thought of my pyramidal stone of Iona, which I had brought along with me as my portable piece of heaven. Supposing it were my task to be an ambassador with a mission to carry a piece of Iona to the King's Chamber, so that the two "stones" should make contact? Crazy as it sounds, I knew that was my answer. I slept well.

The next morning I cannily packed my rucksack with the stone, a pack of peppermints (for coolness of breath), a little bag of cayenne (pyramid pepper!) in case anyone passed out, and a flashlight in case the Egyptian government had a power failure. That, I figured, should cover all contingencies.

A fleet of buses was lined up at the dock to take the "Cheepos" (as a Greek had misdubbed us) to Cairo. We

went to the Cairo museum first. I have to digress here
because it was such a marvelous experience. The museum is a vast cocoa-colored cavern, solemn and silent.
Voices get lost as people speak. I do not believe a speck
of dust had moved an inch since I was there as a child.
The exhibits were powerful, enormously brooding, and
watched over by Egyptian guards who were dwarfed
in every room by the stature of the silent stone figures.
One breathed in the awe of antiquity.

Several floors above, off in a corner room, were selected mummies in various states of undress. Here, the
New Age contingent got to work. Men and women in
our group spread out to measure the energy in the mummy chakras. Solemnly with eyes closed, they moved their
hands up and down a few inches above the corpses. I
remember one mummy, whose skull was bound rather
ludicrously with a bandage holding up his jaw. He had
a rakish look as if to show how much he was enjoying
his psychic massage, finally after all these millennia!
There happened to be some French tourists in the room.
Their eyes were practically popping out! *"Mais, qu'est
qu'ils font? C'est fou!"* What were we doing, how crazy
could we be! These Americans, these Americans! I myself
had brought an aurameter along, a metal device on a
spring. Secretly, with some embarrassment, I tried it
on a golden casket. It went wild and freaked out the
Egyptian guard. I've never been able to repeat the experiment because, short of Fort Knox, I haven't had access to that much solid gold. You have to remember that
I was an Easterner and not as ready as the Californians
to accept so much without skepticism. I used to remark
that if and when the great earthquake were to hit California, it wouldn't hurt the people because they were

already three feet off the ground anyway. (Then I moved to California myself!)

Later we set off for Gizeh, winding through a much-changed Cairo with modern hotels, wide streets, and billboards advertising Japanese products. Here and there I would spot an old horse carriage left over from my childhood days. Once out into the countryside and along the Nile, it all looked familiar. The *fellahin* in their caftans, the goats and camels, the women washing clothes in the river canals, the storks wheeling overhead. And the heat! By the time we reached the desert, it was 105 degrees.

Since this was such a large group with a serious purpose, Maggie Smith had arranged with the government to clear the area for a while of souvenir hawkers and even other tourists. The elderly had an option to drive from the Sphinx up to the Great Pyramid. I was tempted, but decided against it. So, with Brugh and Rosalyn at the head of the line, we climbed in a long serpentine row through the heavy sands, up and up towards our goal. The magnificent outline of the three pyramids towered up against a blazing blue sky. Again I remembered the sight of them as a child mounted on a white donkey called Beautiful Night, and my parents rocking high on camels. A sandstorm had suddenly come, whipping the sand against my legs so cruelly that I cried, and everyone, including the camels, had had to turn their backs and cover their heads.

This time when I reached the entrance to the pyramid, the people who were first were already coming out. So that everyone would have a chance to see it, we had

been asked to stay no more than ten minutes in the King's
Chamber. I noticed that those emerging were all covered
with sweat. Their faces were red from exertion and their
clothes stuck to their bodies. I myself could already feel
trickles of moisture running down my back and my legs.
It was time for the peppermints. I offered one to Bill
Davis, who was behind me. He was a physicist from
NASA, and to him I confided my apprehensions. He
kindly volunteered to stay right behind me and to en-
courage me. He did, too. Edith Wallace went in and
wisely came out immediately. It was not for her at her
age.

I remembered the stone of Iona and clambered into
the darkness. The air was indeed fetid and slightly cooler
than that outside but still exeedingly hot. We immediately began the arduous ascent, up, and up and up through
the tunneled passages lit here and there with flickering
fluorescent rods. The group now began to chant, and
whispered instructions were passed down not to talk idly
or giggle, but to observe the ritual nature of what we
were doing. Between Bill Davis and Woodstock, my
stick, I managed to get to the Queen's Chamber. The
way was too long to crawl on all fours, and too low to
stand up. The exertion for a person my size was fierce,
and may have contributed to what was to follow. After
the Queen's Chamber came the Big Step. Here Brugh
stood at the ready to help those like me to climb it. He
smiled cheerfully. Then came the ascent to the King's
Chamber, which involved climbing up a gangplank
while others' rumps were coming down. The chanting
swelled above and below.

Bill remembers, as I do, two men bypassing us on the
right side. They seemed to be in a hurry. One was

dressed in blue and the other in brown. I assumed that
they were reporters or officials. When we got up into
the dimly lit chamber, there were about forty people
sitting or standing. Rosalyn was at the entrance, anoint-
ing us on the forehead with oil as we came in. I remember her smile as she decided to anoint Woodstock as well.
Her husband was wearing a white sailor's cap, which
seemed a bit incongruous. The chanting was continuous,
and Bill and I sat with our backs against the wall. Some
people were climbing in and out of the empty sarcoph-
agus, but I felt for the stone of Iona and fulfilled my
mission, touching it to the ancient stone of the King's
Chamber. I was flooded with relief, if not euphoria. My
mission was accomplished—a piece of Iona was now
connected with this awesome place. I was just plum happy, and after some minutes squeezed Bill's hand and
whispered that I would go down now. He wanted to
stay a bit longer.

I got up and made my way to the doorway. There
stood a man in a blue suit, a white shirt and a necktie.
He was wearing polished black shoes. I looked into his
friendly pink face, and noticed his white hair and kindly
smile. He looked exceedingly Celtic, like a shorter Alis-
tair Cooke, and I was sorry that I had not seen him
before aboard ship. He reached out a warm hand,
smiled, bowed a little, and said quite formally, "How
wonderful it is to see you here, Alice!" And he covered
my hand with both of his. I laughed and told him frankly
of my fears that I would never make it. He laughed,
too, and I promised myself to seek him out again when
we got back to the boat.

I fairly floated all the way down, though I know it
involved a descent as hot and sweaty as the way up.

Finally I reached the entrance, where an old Egyptian attendant sitting at a table made a point of admiring the amber beads I was wearing. He rolled them in his fingers, murmuring something, and then looked sharply and knowingly into my eyes. He knew.

The bus was air-conditioned when I climbed into it, and someone mercifully handed me a Coke. Shortly thereafter, Bill climbed in and we shared it. I kept thinking about the man in the blue suit. What was it about him that made him stick in my mind? Then it hit me. Every single one of us was dripping with sweat, rumpled, and wringing wet. He had been immaculate, without a trace of perspiration or a hair out of place. So I began to ask Bill and then the others if they had noticed him. Not one had, nor was the delightful gentleman on board the ship.

Finally, I asked Rosalyn, who had been standing only a few feet away from him. "Oh, yes," she replied. "That was Dr. Johnson. He came to supervise, in case of any medical emergency." I pressed further. Dr. Johnson, it seemed, was a physician who had left this world over a hundred years ago. He was one of Rosalyn's guides. For me, though, he was a Scotsman thanking me for bringing the stone of Iona.

You shook your head, and we both looked out the window across to the twinkling lights of Fionnphort on the other side of the water. Yes, I told you, I had shared the story with Fritjof Capra. He believed me, bless him, but could come up with no explanation. I assured him that I was not psychic. Intuitive, yes, because of the

nature of my work, but not psychic. This Dr. Johnson's
hand was as real as my own. For me he was no appari-
tion. All I can think is that, helped by the reputed power
of the pyramid and my own euphoric condition, my consciousness was raised a dimension, which had enabled
him to come down to meet me at that instant. Whatever
the cause, when something like that actually happens
it forces you to rearrange a lot of furniture in your head.
It has left me with the feeling that many of our most
common assumptions about reality are hypotheses.

No, I have not seen him since, but I can't think of
anything nicer than stepping over the threshold at the
end of my life to find his arm extended and him smiling the while and saying, "How wonderful it is to find
you here, Alice!"

We sat quietly, listening to the British voices discreetly
rising and falling around us in the lounge. As we discovered later, both of us were thinking the same thought:
because of the success of that Chi-ops trip, another one
was mounted the next year. The ship sailed this time
from Venice, and the first night aboard you were invited by Maggie Smith to join us at our table. You sat
down beside me and we began a conversation which has
gone on ever since. Sometimes we cannot help but wonder at fate managing to connect two people who lived
on opposite coasts of the United States by uniting them
on the glistening night sea of the Mediterranean. For
two weeks a courtship ensued, accompanied by 400 in-
dulgent chaperones. We did all the things that the most
glamorous advertisements of cruises speak of—leaned
over the railing in our evening clothes, watched the

moonlit wake of the ship in the warm evening breezes. We danced and held hands. The only irony was our white hair and our age. Perhaps the blessing is that by now we had learned the secret of happiness is to know when you are happy. To appreciate and give thanks.

If my idea of heaven was to be on Iona, it was you who were making it real.

There is a tree
that grows in me
a tree
that no one else can see.
There is a bird
upon the tree
upon the tree
that grows in me.
The tree that no one else can see.
And when the bird
upon the tree
begins to sing
you think it's me.
                    Karla Kuskin, Something's
                         Sleeping in the Hall

The tree symbolizes the individua-
tion process in the sense of living
one's own life and thereby becoming
conscious of the self, i.e., gnosis.
                    Marie-Louise von Franz

FIBONACCI AT THE KITCHEN DOOR

Fronds of one stock furl
mathematically considerate
of each other's surging into space,
their rectitude
the straightest line in nature,
their modesty in touching curl
of heads bowed
in proportion's acknowledgement
of place.

I am undone, dear Fibonacci,
by this green and silent sermon
of humble harmony's
return.
An old testament of ordered law —
a new testament of beauteous portent —
a family of fern.
                              A.O.

IV

ᴄrees

The next day we set forth again on a ramble, headed for a climb. You were still mulling over the matter of the stone in the pyramid. "You aren't suggesting that that particular stone was 'magic,' were you?"

"No, not at all! The power of the stone was what I projected onto it. It was all that it meant to me, the meaning I gave to it. I could throw it back into the ocean and it would roll around there for thousands of years, both special and unspecial like any other stone. In fact, the alchemists said something to the effect that the Philosopher's Stone could not be bought for any price, and it might lie under the feet of people and wagons in the street. The power in the stone really lay in the alchemist himself. The transmutations, I suspect, are the very lifting of the meaning of life from one level to another, both outwardly and inwardly in the psyche. Such transmutations are everywhere in nature, but discovering the hidden processes requires a certain kind of symbolic thinking that puts two and two together—which, by the way, is what *symbolus* means. What helped me so greatly was discovering that key in astrology. This was the great de-

coder or 'algebra of life' for me, and I tried to share it
in my book *Jungian Symbolism in Astrology.*"

You asked me if I could give a more specific example. Suddenly, I remembered a dream I had had of Jung:

> Jung is lighting his pipe with a match. He is wearing an
> old tweed jacket. Between puffs he says: "Alice, did you
> know there is only one plant that grows in both our
> worlds?" He looks at me sharply. I am taken aback, but
> think to myself that if ever there were an opportunity
> to ask him, it was now. "No," I say with the hopeful
> gleam of a schemer in my eye, "what is it?" Jung shakes
> out the match and winks at me. "Oh, you'll recognize
> it when you see it."

Then I woke up. After several years, I have some suspi-
cions as to what he might have meant.

Now it was your turn. "Well, what is it?"

And I grinned, "You'll see!"

We continued our walk north of the abbey. It was
a Thursday, which meant it was a boat day, a day when
the Caledonian MacBrayne steamer would round Mull,
having passed Fingal's Cave, and would be met by our
small ferry, which would then ply to and fro landing
hundreds of pilgrims onto Iona. Some serious, some just
for a day's outing; old, young, married, single; British,
Asiatic, American, European; all would push forward
in an eager, friendly crowd and then break up to feel
their way separately. It was a good day for Dun I, the
highest point on the island and the spot up to which Columba climbed to make sure that he could no longer see
the coast of Ireland. Some say he was angry at his com-

patriots because he had not been allowed to keep the copy of the gospels he had worked on for so long. In fact, a battle was fought over the book, and a trial held, at which the following was adjudicated: "To every cow its calf, to every book its copy." So put out was Columba by this ruling that he vowed never to set foot on Irish soil again. And later, when he had to return, they say he put sand from Iona in his shoes to be sure he didn't touch ground!

Though the rough pyramidal hill is only 300 feet high, it took quite a while, and a fair amount of huffing and puffing on my part, to get to the top, since there was no path. But I was thinking of a way to answer your question, nevertheless. Finally we reached the summit, removed our parkas, and sat down with our backs to the cairn built by climbers over the years. The view was magnificent, with the sea surrounding our very small island stretching in all directions. Far below we could see little white dots of sheep, some black and white spots which were cows, a laundry line of clothes, and the many figures of ambling pilgrims who would not have time to climb Dun I. We shared a thermos of hot tea and two cheese rolls, then leaned back in the cool warmth of the sun.

I suppose, I said, that I first learned of all this from my teacher M, whom I had met when I was twenty-one and wrote of in my first book. His message seemed to be that we can only see half of anything; the other half is the meaning that we give to what we see. To demonstrate, he had put a child's block in front of me and asked me what I saw. "A block, a cube," I'd said. "How many sides can you see?" "Three." "How many sides to a block?" "Six." "How do you know there are six, if you only see three?" "I just know." "Who supplied the other three sides?" I'd had to admit that I did.

Next time, I told you, we were in the country and looking at a most beautiful apple tree. It was laden with clustered fruit. We sat down on the grass and M lay back on one elbow. "Close your eyes," he instructed, "and tell me how that tree came into being, and with every step you describe, see how it might apply to any of us." I closed my eyes.

A.O.: It starts with an apple pip.

M: Become the apple pip.

A.O.: I am below ground. Dark, alone, cold, not much hope.

M: Good. What next?

A.O.: I think I split in four ways. My sides open out, a rootlet goes down, and a shootlet goes up. I feel like a cross. It's like a death, almost. I don't know why I am doing this. I suppose it's geotropism?

M: What is geotropism?

A.O.: You know, reaching for the sun, reaching for the light.

M: Put that in human terms. What do you tell me you have been reaching for these last eight years? All that hullaballoo!

A.O.: For understanding, for God, whatever that means.

M: What is the seed telling you?

A.O.: That you have to go down before you can go up. You have to be grounded, rooted. [I'd had to grin, being forced to admit this, since this was my own problem.]

M: What would happen if you weren't?

A.O.: I'd blow away and dry up.

M: How many elements do you feel?

A.O.: Earth, water, a little fire—

M: Where's the fire?

A.O.: In me, I suppose. I am alive.

M: Where did the fire come from?

A.O.: From the tree that bore me? And the one before that and on and on. I guess I am lucky.

M: What next?

A.O.: I grow up through the surface of the earth. It is very, very different now. Space! Air! Warmth! and I discover I am not alone.

M: A new element. You are now on another level. Do you hear what I am saying? Would it be easy for you to describe this to the other seeds below ground?

A.O.: They wouldn't believe me! They just have to trust and reach like I did.

M: Do you see the sun?

A.O.: No, I feel it. But as I grow and grow up towards it, a lot of complications set in.

M: Like what?

A.O.: Weather! Rain, cold, snow. I think I had some leaves and they all fell off!

M: Never mind. Winter is a sleep time. Keep growing. Go forward several years. What now?

A.O.: I keep reaching up, but I keep going sideways into branches and twigs and leaves.

M: What could that mean?

A.O.: The more leaves I have, the stronger I grow.

M: Put that in human terms.

A.O.: That's hard. Maybe it means that to make a mistake is to expose a greater surface to experience. The branches make loops in another direction, at an angle to the trunk of the tree.

M: What do leaves do for a tree?

A.O.: They hold out their hands to the sun. Photosynthesis?

M: That's right. They deal directly with the sun, each one absorbing what light it can.

A.O.: You mean like when we make a mistake and learn something.

M: (gently) It doesn't always have to be a mistake. Just having a genuine attack of insight will do it.

A.O.: You mean an "Aha!" So every leaf makes wisdom. Why, the whole tree is full of "ahas!"

M: Aha! (laughing, in spite of himself) I think you're learning something. Keep on growing a few more years, what will happen next?

A.O.: I will bloom. I will be filled with blossoms, fragrance, and birds will sing in my branches. I will know God and make love with the sun.

M: What would that be in human terms?

A.O.: Love? Samadhi? Communion? It's hard to even talk about it.

M: Are you on another level, perhaps?

A.O.: Yes.

M: Can you stay there? What happens next?

A.O.: No. About a week. And then a breeze blows all the petals away.

M: Then what happens?

A.O.: Little green apples where the blossoms were. It will take forever for them to ripen!

M: What are they?

A.O.: Our gifts? Our experience?

M: Can you keep them? Are they yours?

A.O.: No, they fall off where others can take them. But I can make more.

M: Is that another level?

A.O.: Yes.

M: Now, can you see that this is one tree and yet there are many levels of process within it?

A.O.: Yes, each is different.

M: What do they all have in common? This is hard. Think before you answer. Remember, you are still in first grade here! This exercise can yield more and more and more understanding as you grow older.

A.O.: Well, the sun, and the moon, and the day and the night, and the seasons circle around. And the sap of the tree is circulating. The mineral kingdom is turning into the vegetable kingdom. And if you eat an apple, it will become animal, and human. The four elements: air, fire, earth and water are involved, literally and symbolically. The unseen roots, which don't get much credit, will have grown as large and wide as the tree, I expect.

M: And on another level?

A.O.: You mean the process of reproduction? Children? Poems? Paintings?

M: Where in your studies have you come across trees?

A.O.: The Garden of Eden? Yggdrasil, the tree that Odin hung on? Druids. The Christmas Tree. Sometimes they say Christ hung on a tree.

M: Dearie (and he put his hand on my arm), you will discover many more trees, and they all mirror the One Living Tree, the one you already have within you.

"And did he tell you what it was?" you asked. No! Like Jung in the dream, he left it for me to recognize. But he did get up and pick two apples. One he gave to me, and the other he sliced in half sideways. He asked if I knew what I would see in there. I had never cut an apple that way. It looked like this:

"That is a pentagram," he told me, "the symbol of knowledge. The mathematical proportions of that, as well as the geometric ones, have kept philosophers busy ever since the ancient Greeks. Someday, you will study this and learn how well God geometrizes. You see, Wisdom knew just what the Creator would enjoy! In every apple, every snowflake, every flower and crystal, everywhere in nature, wherever you look and *learn how to see*, there is an aha! waiting. Scientists down through the ages observe and study nature. They accomplish wonderful things, but too often they are looking only with their brilliant minds. They forget that they are only seeing half. They do not connect it with themselves or see their knowledge as steps towards meaning, steps to what you call God. This was the direction the old alchemists were taking, but they had to work in secret. It was too dangerous in those days to suggest that divinity could be hidden in this world. But Wisdom is not hidden. She is everywhere, but she hides like a dove in a stone." Years later I was to come across a reference in an alchemical work which spoke of "the dove hidden in foliated earth."

My throat was dry after so long a discussion. Generously, you handed me the last swig of warm tea, and we got up and stretched. You smiled happily and took my hand to help me down. "That was the Tree of Life, wasn't it!"

We clambered further. It was far trickier going down. In the distance we could see the ferry taking the last of the pilgrims back to the mother ship. When we reached level ground, you turned and asked me if I still had the poem called "The Poles of Eden." I would have to look.

When we came to the abbey, the flock of white doves was circling over its slated roof, white against a gathering dark, but their wings were shot with gold from the slanting late afternoon sun.

Back to the hotel. Time for a "Scottish communion," the wee dram mindfully shared before the supper to come.

Later I looked for the poem and found it among my notes. As I read it through again, I saw more and more what it was trying to say about the Tree of Life growing within us, Jung's plant that grows in both our worlds. So I gave it to you, and sitting in the simplicity of our hotel bedroom, the words rolled back over my memory, words of meaning that I now found a deeper understanding of than when they had come to me.

THE POLES OF EDEN

Do not let me mock you, dear
do not let me hope
do not let me gather
    a mother and a father
    nor ask them why
after the release of gold
after the silver of their peace
after the sadness and the sleep
    they gave up, turned inward
    each to each his leaden dream
and left you weeping in their deep
      crying
        screaming
          shuddering
for comfort and for love to keep.

Godself has a great pair of pincers
    half, a woman

half, a man
and where they close, were one and One
in pulsing pinch of promise
        life begins, and love began.

Oh, constant Adam, taste your apple
roll your tongue about those pips
and kiss sweet knowing Eve
upon her musing lips
        her womb will render
        sons and pentacles and steer
                and chattel is what those sons
                will hold most dear—

spliced and sliced out of spit and soil and split
One into desperate two
you seek through sweat and shame
and serpent dream, and do—
        and you, poor Eve, aborted all that pain
        that Self might gain in Abel and in Cain
                and Adam called you keening
                back to rest—you were his soul
                his hope, your breast
                and Seth he rendered second
                unto death.

Tell me, son, still young
and brown, and marked, and hairy,
do you range the desert?
are you lonely?
do you range
where stone and spirit
make exchange?
        if you quest and thirst and rave
        for answers, seek the mountain
        seek the fountain
        in that initiating cave—

there you'll find a tomb will mouth
your prick of conscience

and swallow continents and questions
the pestilence of thinking
deeds and fears

> *you'll pass through such a death of seed to peace*
> *where one in beauty bends to save*
> *to lead you up bright step*
> *to nightwebbed gossamer*
> *to what you crave*

and at that inner height
you'll find from apple's pride and root
from knowledge and from apple tomb absolved
grown
now luminous, now numinous
your flowering Tree of Light
your sanctifying Fruit of Light—

Godself holds a branch of annulating fire
and flails his grain
with time and with desire

> *and when all and ever*
> *will be spent*
> *retted and rent*

He'll gather from the chaff and ash, the spark
and spin it starwards up
to spiral out to shimmer in the dark

> *then rest and smile*
> *know and be charmed by love*
> *filled and fulfilled*

for this
> *ah, yes,*
> > *is Wisdom.*

This is what She meant.

                                                  A.O.

The secret of the spirit is, of course, not the sole prerogative of Celtic spirituality. Because it is forever unquenchable, it has flared like a burning bush in Western spirituality, even in ages when Western eyes since the seventeenth century were becoming so mesmerized by physical reality that they seemed incapable any longer of looking through it to that which lay hidden and which called beyond it.
                                   Herbert O'Driscoll

A man that looks on glasse
On it may stay his eye
Or if he pleaseth, through it passe
And then the heav'n espie.
                                   George Herbert,
                                       "The Elixir"

It is interesting to see expressed the feeling of common creation. However this is very far removed from any sort of easy-going, romantic pantheism. At the heart of this sense of unity lies the recognition that everything good comes from God and is to be given freedom to be itself, to enjoy and be enjoyed, and that we are enslaved if we care for anything that excludes the Giver.
    Esther de Waal, "God under my Roof"

Make it so that time is a circle and not a line.
                                   Simone Weil

V

Crosses

It was raining hard the next morning when we woke up. Looking out the window, I noticed that Mull and almost all of the sound had disappeared into a nimbic grey, which made the patch of green lawn and the hedges more brilliant green. We hastened to dress because we had agreed to attend an early service at the Bishop's House, which was the Episcopalian Church of Scotland. Due to the country's complex religious history, Columba's abbey, which had been established in Catholic times, was now Protestant and Presbyterian. There is yet another kirk on the island, the Iona Parish Church of the local residents, for the abbey currently is an international center, since the Iona Community was founded to serve the youth of inner cities, and to promote peace, social justice, and the equality of women in the world. As an understanding had been reached among the Presbyterians, a fourth church of the Wee Frees had been relinquished and was now the home of our hotel owners, and surrounded by the normal paraphernalia of a growing family. Somehow for me this epitomized symbolically the fusion of sacred and secular.

We geared up in our mackintoshes and newly acquired Wellies and set off valiantly before breakfast and coffee. Not that we had far to go, only down the road towards the jetty and then left along a wee path between garden walls. The rain really was pelting us, pattering on our hoods, forcing us to look down. Every stone and pebble was washed and bright, and every breath of air was filled with a cool green sweetness. We met two philosophical, black-faced sheep cropping away at the edge of the path, a ewe and her overgrown lamb. We exchanged greetings. Despite the weather, everything felt "entirely grand," as they say in Ireland. I thought to myself, I must be looking with a loving eye!

The small chapel within the Bishop's House was as intimate and feminine as the abbey was lofty and stone-great. A slender crucifix stood upon a block of Iona marble on the altar, and wooden figures of Mary and Joseph, attended by wildflowers, sheltered in window niches on either side. The few of us who had arrived were crinkled and crunched in our raingear, and you could not miss the rosy cheeks of the men and women coming in out of the cold and wet. The service itself was traditional and familiar. I remembered that George Seabury, the first American Episcopal bishop, was ordained in Scotland since he had been refused by the English, due to their hard feelings about the American Revolution. The line of the "apostolic succession," that ceremonial laying-on of hands of one generation of priests upon the next, going all the way back to St. Peter in Rome made it impossible for me to escape a sense of history at this moment. The serious young priest before us (otherwise an avid fisherman), stood next in the line of succession.

I confess my mind wandered back to the classroom where I had struggled to make history come alive for

the sixth graders it had been my good fortune to teach.
"How many 'touches' away do you suppose you are from
George Washington?" I asked them. Well, not as many
as you think. When my father was a little boy, he was
taken to the World's Fair in St. Louis, and at that fair
was a booth where there sat a very, very old black man
to whom you could pay a nickel for a handshake. This
man's father had been a slave on Washington's planta-
tion and he had proudly let George Washington hold
his son, then a baby. Now my own father had sat on
his lap. So, from Washington to the old man was one
touch, to my father was two, and to me, three. Only
three bodies stood between my students and the found-
ing father of our country! I was giving them fourth
touches as they eagerly stretched out their hands. Now
they could run home and give fifth touches to others.
Since my father was always meeting interesting people,
I was also only two touches from such as Mark Twain,
Eisenhower, Queen Elizabeth, Goering, etc., etc. (I
myself had been forced to sit in Mussolini's lap.) The
next day, the kids came in to give me touches from all
kinds of celebrities themselves. This exercise made history
far more immediate. The apostolic succession is really
the same process carried out formally and consciously.
Perhaps the Christian ritual had started out as what the
yogis call *shaktipat*, the physical transmission of spiritual
awakening.

I now paid attention to the service again while admiring the flowered altar cloth, the deep blue tapestry
reredos, and the quiet radiance of the crucifix. It dif-
fered from the Celtic crosses outside and inside the abbey and from those all over Scotland and Ireland, for
that matter, for it was a simple cross. The Celtic cross

has a circle added, a fact which led you and me to another interesting conversation later on.

After friendly exchanges we left the chapel and headed for that cup of coffee, our porridge, and kippers. Since it was still raining, we agreed to write some postcards, walk to the post office, and eat at the little restaurant near the jetty.

The few hours sped by. We soon found ourselves at a table looking out at the fog and listening to rock-and-roll and the chatter of the young women in the kitchen preparing sandwiches and soup for lunch—their chatter a lively singsong of Gaelic mixed with English. Otherwise we had the place to ourselves. And I had brought paper and pencils in case the Muse struck.

Actually, it was you who brought up the matter of the crosses. Of all the stone symbols on Iona, they are the most striking. These great high crosses, like those in Ireland, are elaborately carved with Celtic interlacings, touching figures, and animals. On Iona there are three: Maclean's Cross, St. John's and St. Martin's. And, when you come to think of it, there are so many different variations on the basic simple design, such as the Jerusalem, the trefolated, St. Andrew's, the swastika and Lorraine crosses, to mention only a few. What made crosses so compelling that Jung would remark that even the most ignorant peasant gazing at one in a church would benefit from its healing effect? Is it because they stand for the crucifixion, or is it because the sign of the cross has been the icon of the Age of Pisces (roughly 5 B.C.-1800 A.D., not counting interfaces)? Perhaps it represents a profound collective message concerning our own necessary sacrifice of ego. The cross basically is a symbol of quaternity and totality speaking directly to the psyche long before the advent of Christian culture. "But how can you prove it?" you asked.

"Well," I answered, "this is where astrology and sacred geometry can help." We cleared away the tea cups and out came the paper and pencils. And I was reminded of one of those dumb, doomed-to-be unanswered questions I asked as a child: "How come when you stand up, you are awake, but when you lie down to sleep you're flat?" Aha! as M would say.

I shared with you that sacred or esoteric geometry is not only interesting, it is fun. Ironically, I used to bemoan the hours lost with Euclid in a boring classroom, day after day, with one equally bored Miss Morse. To date, I've only applied what I had learned in a practical way once, and that was when I made my three daughters matching skating skirts out of red felt. However, since I stumbled onto esoteric geometry, Miss Morse has been many times blessed, for, indisputably, geometry is yet another way in which the sacred and the commonplace connect and fuse. Through it the logical mind and a nautilus shell become one, and the archetypal patterns in the unconscious become lattices already crystallized in nature.

We know already that in sacred geometry, the cube stands for the manifest, for matter. This symbolism was ubiquitous in medieval thinking, and in Kabbalism, as well as in the "secret doctrine." You find it in the Tarot, and it is alluded to in Renaissance painting, to say nothing of alchemy. Now, when you take a cube, it points

Primer of Sacred Geometry — two dimensions

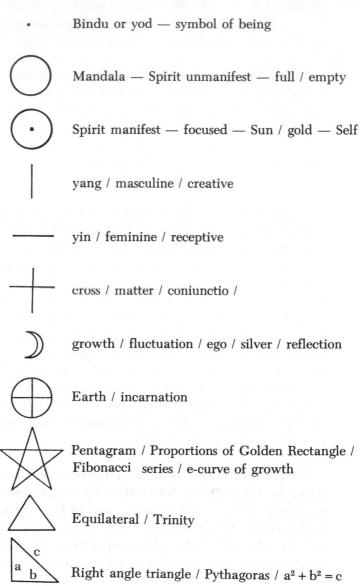

Bindu or yod — symbol of being

Mandala — Spirit unmanifest — full / empty

Spirit manifest — focused — Sun / gold — Self

yang / masculine / creative

yin / feminine / receptive

cross / matter / coniunctio /

growth / fluctuation / ego / silver / reflection

Earth / incarnation

Pentagram / Proportions of Golden Rectangle / Fibonacci series / e-curve of growth

Equilateral / Trinity

Right angle triangle / Pythagoras / $a^2 + b^2 = c$

Square / that which can be measured

Tetraktys / $1 + 2 + 3 + 4$ / $1 \times 2 \times 3 \times 4$

Lemniscate / eternity

All further figures can be drawn using only
a compass and a right angle — ponder them.

to the six directions: north, south, east, west, up and
down. A cube is three-dimensional. If you were to un-
fold it, you would have a cross. This is two-dimensional.

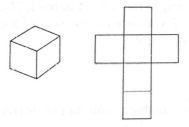

The great symbol of totality is the circle or mandala.
In sacred geometry the circle without a dot is *spirit un-*
manifest, the circle with a dot focusing the center is *spirit*
manifest. It is the Sun (for primordial thinkers a symbol for God), and for Jung a symbol for the Self, which
he described as the center and totality of the individual
psyche. The circle alone is the Great Unknowable. Why?
Because its area can never be known. Why? Because of
the nature of pi. $A = \pi r^2$ is the formula for the area of
a circle. And, thanks to the ancient Sumerians, we know
that a circle has 360 degrees.

"So far so good?" You nodded. Simple. Obvious.

All right then. I asked you how you can prove geometrically that wherever you have a cross, an invisible circle is implied. Which would be asking, philosophically, how you can prove that wherever there is matter, spirit is invisibly present. I drew the cross on the paper and you leaned over with pursed lips to study it.

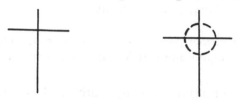

"Hmmm. I don't see it, but I know it's there. Is that it?" You looked again and then, aha! you made mine into a Celtic cross. "That's it," I agreed, "but prove it." Another pause. Back to Miss Morse and Euclid. "How many angles are there?"

"Four."

"Right angles, at that. How many degrees in a right angle?"

Your face broke into a smile—90 degrees, and 4 x 90 = 360.

"But that's not all," I grinned back. "In astrological and in sacred geometry, a vertical line is a yang line, creative; and a horizontal one is a yin line, receptive."

Sometimes, in teaching astrology to therapists familiar with Jung, I will draw a horizontal line, a time line for a human life. On it one can mark the physical milestones of birth, puberty, sex and reproduction, death.

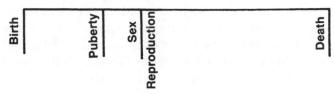

At the same time, I describe my definition of how you know if you or your patient is identified with his or her ego. It's when we describe reality as just one damn thing after another! You get born, go to school, get a job, get hitched, have kids, work until you retire, move to Florida and kick the bucket! Maybe buy one of those tee shirts that proclaim, "Life's a bitch and then you die." By the way, once I drew this line when a Tibetan lama was present who commented that the English language makes antonyms of life and death. Birth and death are the antonyms, and both are part of a greater life, and he drew a circle around the line. This was very comforting to me.

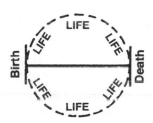

All religions of the world, including the most primitive ones, make these basic physical rites of passage sacred by inviting the god(s) to participate in them.

When this happens, a birth becomes a baptism or a Brith Milah; puberty, a Bar Mitzvah or confirmation or vision quest; and so forth. By drawing the cross one has invited one's greater Self to participate in the daily life led by the ego. And in so doing, a *coniunctio* or *hierosgamos,* an inner sacred marriage, takes place within the psyche. Life becomes greater than life, and the sacred has entered our everyday life. This is the secret of the "union of opposites," and the symbolism implicit in fairy tales and parables, myths and alchemy, of the marriage of the King and the Queen, the gold and the silver, the Sun and the Moon, or in the psyche, the Self and the ego, and in life, the sacred and the commonplace. Through consciously making "the sign of the cross" the invisible circle is invoked.

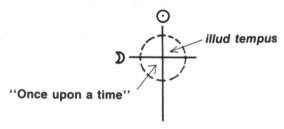

Now that "magic circle" is also a way of demonstrating something about sacred time and space. Jung used special terms for magic time or time out of time. For him it was *illud tempus* or *in illo tempore* (and I always suspect that the Self speaks Latin and Greek!). He meant *that* time or what we would call "once upon a time," which is always *now* and the time the psyche lives in. It is also at that very centerpoint of crossing where the flash of synchronicity occurs and the *unus mundus* or one world is revealed, so that an outer event coincides exactly with an inner state or meaning. The beautiful part is that any of us, Christian or not, can make this "sign of the cross" more consciously by touching the Third Eye and drawing our hand down to the heart or solar plexus, inviting God as the Divine Guest to participate in our horizontal quotidian life lived by the ego, as we draw the line between our shoulders. (Shoulders are ruled by the sign Gemini, which also rules daily life!)

Whenever we sustain that *illud tempus* even for a short time, life acquires a magical intensity, the syntropy I wrote of in my previous book. It ceases to wind down entropically into a drag, but revs up to another level. This is the level that the Masters live on all the time.

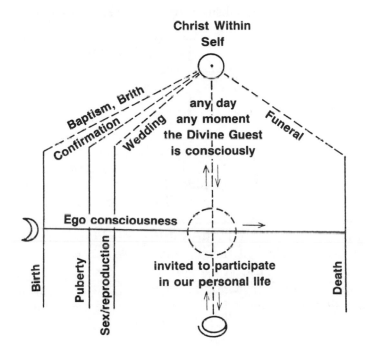

Individuation as Incarnation

This must be why the simplest thing that Jesus did has become suffused with message and meaning ever since. Many people have spoken to women at wells, but *that* conversation transcends time for Christians, as Gautama's encounter with the distraught mother and her dead baby transcends time for Buddhists. And both of them increasingly so for all of us. At a secular level it is what distinguishes a "classic" book, play, painting or piece of music from an ordinary creation pervaded by *l'air du temps*. Such a work has an archetypal import that transcends time. It is the reason that myths and fairy tales, those collective "classics," survive even the hardest times, those of rationalism and so-called Enlightenment.

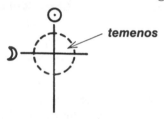

If we look at the "magic circle" again, in terms of space, we have a *temenos*, the Greek word for temple or sacred space. Such a place is where human beings wish heaven to be on earth. If the Blessed Ones, our teachers, are right, there is no distinction in the *unus mundus* anyway, but in this world of dualities, our consciousness makes all the difference. So a *temenos* becomes, exoterically, a formal place of worship: temple, church, mosque, synagogue, or tepee. But (and this is also significant) esoterically, it can be wherever two or three or more hold hands in genuine love, friendship, and peace, wherever one invites the Beloved to participate in one's joy, be it poached eggs for breakfast, a night of love, or the sight of anything that lifts your soul. The beauty of three white cranes flying against a dark cloud caused Ramakrishna to fall into samadhi. The rescue of a little girl, after three days in a mineshaft, caused a collective clutch in the heart for the little Persephone brought up from Hades.

So many times in counseling sessions, I hear people afraid to speak of happiness, out of a superstitious fear that it will be stolen from them. This is the ego fearing for itself. Yet we turn to God in our pain and anguish with prayers of supplication. So why should we withold our joys, humble as they may be, from the Beloved? That would be as bad as witholding something good from your dearest love or friend! I may sound irreverent, but as I told you, it must get to be a terrible drag for the Divine Guest within us to hear nothing but "bitch, bitch, bitch" all day and *mea culpa, mea culpa* all night. It is as if we keep saying that our lives are too stupid and unworthy for the Beloved to be bothered about, when without that divine presence even the grandest events become as nothing.

Then I apologized to you for getting so excited about it. People were coming in the door looking hungry for lunch. You reminded me of Brother Lawrence's *The Practice of the Presence of God*. We laughed because we loved him so much, we named a monk-like brown plastic container Brother Lawrence in his honor. He held the ice at our wedding lovefeast and presides, as did his namesake, over the activities in our kitchen, always a humble and obliging presence. I was so happy when I found out that you had read this gem written by a lay brother, a cook who lived in Paris in the sixteenth century and felt God closest to him in the heat and bustle amid his pots and pans.

Then off we went back up the hill, agreeing heartily that Iona was certainly a *temenos*, and that it might be *illud tempus* for a nap!

OF WISDOM

The Lord possessed me in the beginning of his way,
  before his works of old.
I was set up from everlasting, from the beginning,
  or ever the earth was.
When there were no depths, I was brought forth;
  when there were no fountains abounding with water.
When he established the heavens, I was there
when he marked out the foundations of the earth,
  then I was by him, as a master workman,
and I was daily his delight. . .
rejoicing in his habitable earth.

The Book of Proverbs (8:22-31)

The Trinity consists of Father, Son,
and Holy Ghost, who is represented
by the dove, the bird of Astarte, and
who in early Christian times was
called Sophia and thought of as
feminine.

C.G.Jung

VI

Wands

It was proving to be a marvelous time for both of us. At breakfast we discussed the current return of the feminine and how spontaneously signs of this were appearing in the collective unconscious, in dreams of people, and in literature generally. Suddenly I remembered two dreams of my own that pointed in this direction. While you were relishing your pungent Loch Fyne kippers, I shared them with you:

> I am walking in a forest with a woman friend. Suddenly we come upon a large hole in the ground. A path leads down. We follow the path and enter a dimly lit circular chamber. The earth walls are entirely imbedded with tree roots. In the center an enormous taproot is suspended from the tree above. We notice that it is slowly dripping water. There is a cup there on a chain. I know now that the water is for healing. Carefully, I catch some of the drops and give them to my friend. She drinks, and in turn collects some for me. We then ascend again by another path to the surface.

"That is like nature's communion," you commented. Which, in turn, brought up the second one:

I am with the man I love. We are standing in a copse, a little clearing in a wood. He is dressed in a Shakespearean manner, in green velvet. "I have something for you," he tells me. And he lifts up a large earthen chalice which is covered with moss and little flowers. [I can still feel the coolness of holding it, and the little flowers between my fingers!] I drink of it and so does he. We are drinking love.

Dreams are fascinating, we agreed. If only they were not so elusive, so difficult to remember! I reminded you of your own about having a conversation of some length with Jung. "That's right," you exclaimed. "And I met a woman to whom I expressed my surprise. I had thought Jung was dead. 'No, no,' she said, 'not at all! Jung is very much alive.'"

We finished our coffee agreeing that to be the case.

"So, where do we go today?" you asked.

"We really haven't been to the nunnery yet. That's where the most flowers are. It's the most feminine," I laughed.

True. Except for the private gardens along the waterfront, one finds mostly wildflowers on Iona, but here in what must have been the cloister of the nunnery are lovely garden flowers. There are some benches there where one can sit in the sun and read, or think, or lose oneself in contemplating the roseate quality of the stones. They really are pink, mixed with bits of green and grey, and give a quite different impression from the strong dark greys inside and outside the abbey. It was not a boat day, so we would have a chance for a peaceful time.

Soon we were settled on a bench in the warm sunlight surrounded by the ruins of St. Mary's, a house of Augustinian nuns, which was probably built around 1200 by Reginald, the son of Somerled, the Lord of the Isles who had freed the Hebrides from Norwegian rule. The first prioress was his sister Bethoc. It must have been a very hard life for them. But then this was a period in history when, for the next three hundred years, a great many remarkable women in Europe would begin to make their voices heard. Women whose names have been all but forgotten, Hildegard von Bingen, Mechtild of Magdeburg, St. Douceline de Digne, to name just a few, the stories of whose works and sacrifices are surfacing again as women claim their right to think about and openly discuss matters of soul and spirit. In fact, the Beguines, about whom I've been reading lately, would have fit right in with these times. In many cases they were "channeling" and bringing answers to questions set by the clergy and, in several cases, by the Pope himself. Their visions and writings were quite extraordinary. But finally Rome must have felt threatened, so they were cruelly suppressed. The idea of anyone having such direct communication with higher realms "without benefit of clergy," must have been too much. But you could say they prefigured the Reformation in this respect. One of the characteristics of the last half of this century is the emergence of women writing, in a vivid and meaningful way, of theological matters; women like Ann Ulanov, Anne Freemantle, and Elaine Pagels, to name but a few, who were preceded by Evelyn Underhill, Esther Harding, and Dr. Marie-Louise von Franz. Now books on a feminine theology are truly proliferating—the works of Jeanne Bolen, Christine Downing, and June Singer come to mind.

The nunnery

You must have been reading my mind, because suddenly you turned and said, "Why, do you think, was it so necessary for the Church Fathers to be so cruel and debasing to women in the early centuries? One of them even asked if women had souls! And poor Hypatia of Alexandria, who was flayed alive at the order of the bishop, Cyril, for continuing to teach men philosophy in her school, and she a pagan, at that! Even Columba, a lady at the hotel told me, kept the women and some cows over there on that island." And you pointed indignantly to the *Eilan nam Ban*, the Isle of the Women.

"I don't know," I answered. Maybe they felt threatened. Maybe the masculine Logos side had to pull itself up out of the Great Mother, just the way young boys have to get away from their mothers today when the time comes. Maybe in their unconscious lurked the archetypal memory of chthonic priestesses of the Great Mother Goddess forcing the castration of her priests, and so having women handle sacraments triggered terrible fears. It really wasn't until the troubadors, and the age of chivalry, that matters improved. And a lot of that was due to the greatly increased worship of Mary. Women have had their ups and downs in history. It would be nice if things could even out! Maybe in the Age of Aquarius we can find peace, and find that men and women need each other. Certainly in persecuting women the way they did, men didn't realize that they were persecuting the feminine in themselves, and in nature, to boot. (It is so easy to forget that whatever you do to someone else, you are doing to yourself at the same time!) But when men did that, they rejected the *anima mundi*, the soul of the earth. No wonder the big

myth of the period was the Quest for the Holy Grail.
It represented the lost feminine.

"That's why that dream of yours seemed such a good
one," you grinned.

Once the magic, as you call it, got lost, science and
rationalism and technology made leaps and bounds. But
a science without a sense of the sacred is limited through
the scientist's identification with his own superior in-
telligence. Maybe Descartes should have gone further
with his idea *Cogito ergo sum* (I think, therefore I am)
and added *nunc ergo scivio Deus est* (now, therefore,
I know God is)! Science is not seen as a more intelligent
way to reach God, but more as a way to control rather
than revere nature. Even agriculture is now a matter
of commercial production—wheat, meat, and eggs are
all mass-produced, packaged and dispatched for prof-
it. Nobody seems to care if the egg comes from a happy
hen, scratching busily about. The eggs come from
poultry scrunched in cages, with the lights on all night,
and they roll down into a gutter and get collected and
shipped. The Ember Days are gone when the priest
would circle the fields, followed by the people, praying for favorable weather or giving thanks for the
harvest. The Celts had special prayers for almost everything, from laying a fire, to fishing, or shearing the
sheep. One of my favorites is "The Clipping Blessing,"
which sounds lovely even translated:

> *Go shorn and come woolly*
> *Bear the Beltane female lamb*
> *Be the lovely Brid thee endowing*
> *And the fair Mary thee sustaining*
> *   The fair Mary sustaining thee...*

or "The Consecration of the Seed," which begins like
this:

> *I will go out to sow the seed,*
> *In name of Him that gave it growth;*
> *I will place my front to the wind*
> *And throw a gracious handful on high.*
> *Should a grain fall on a bare rock,*
> *It shall have no soil in which to grow;*
> *As much as falls into the earth*
> *The dew will make it to be full.*

It's as if they invited the Sacred to participate in all
that they did. Now comparatively fewer people live this
way, which is sad. Certainly it remains an ideal for those
in many religions, including the Native American Indian. But how many today, as Jung asked, are really
living a symbolic life, something which gives even the
poorest of the poor a sense of dignity and worth, and
the lack of which robs many who are well-to-do of happiness. So often such ideas are brushed off as impractical, a mystic's way of life. I'm not suggesting that all
people are godless, only that for many God is kept safely housed in a church where He belongs, and not woven
intimately into our everyday living. It is this loving intimacy which is feminine in nature, not coming as bolts
from on high, but rising up like sap in all things that
grow and are alive. It is no less divine for being Wisdom.
The Old Testament says that She was before Creation
began and was His helpmate in clothing His thoughts
in form. Devout, practicing Jews still honor this.

"But weren't there exceptions?" you asked. I loved you
for asking. Having been a businessman for so many
years, much of this was new to you, and yet not new.

I, in turn, envied your practical acumen. We really were working on sharing wits!

Of course there were and are exceptions! Back in the Middle Ages and the Renaissance, the alchemists were the exception, because their real and genuine purpose was spiritual, for they were trying to prove that spirit was hidden in nature as Wisdom. Some of them even suggested that Holy Wisdom or *Hagia Sophia* was the Third Person in the Trinity—that the Holy Ghost was feminine. Which is why its symbol, even today in Christianity, remains the dove. This was sheer heresy in those days, pantheism, and people got burned at the stake for merely suggesting such an idea. But maybe Joachim of Floris was right, and maybe *this* New Age will be the Age of the Holy Ghost, and maybe we will discover that the reemergence of the feminine, not in anger but in Wisdom, is what's to come. If we could somehow prove to mankind that our earth itself has a soul, and that it is weeping, maybe that would help. Maybe someday science, the new science, will prove what the mystics throughout the ages have always known: matter has consciousness. Matter is consciousness with form; nature is energy expressed through form in beauty.

It could be that simple. The trouble is, most people would think we were nuts. So we have to sacrifice caring if they do. Again, it must be a matter of levels. I once was told that an atheist is simply a person who has rejected the image of god on the level below him and gotten stuck. And there are levels and levels, as my teacher told me.

"What we need," you said flat out with a big sigh, "is a magic wand! Something to tap people on the head with and wake them up!" Well, that's exactly what Hagia Sophia is all about, though expressed in far more lofty terms. After all, respect is due the Holy Trinity.

"But," you protested, "isn't that just the point, and why we keep missing it! Wasn't the Holy Ghost also called the Paraclete, the Comforter? Wasn't Sophia the one who, at the time of creation, hid herself playfully from God in matter, as drops of light? Wasn't Wisdom said to be kind and cheerful? I can look it up in Jung's *Answer to Job* back at the hotel. Why did they get rid of Hagia Sophia?"

Actually, the Russian and Greek Orthodox Churches never did. In fact, they have always kept her tradition profoundly alive. The Russian writers Vladimir Solovyov, Pavel Florensky, and Mikhail Bulgakov have written most beautifully about her. It was Western Christianity that seemingly forgot her.

Hagia Sophia means "Holy Wisdom" in Greek. Perhaps when this got translated into Latin, it became *spiritus sanctus,* and since the words are of masculine endings, all the referring pronouns became "he" and "him." Latin was for centuries the written language of the educated in the West and, until just recently, the official language of the Roman Catholic Church. Language can shape our thinking, and perhaps people just ended up with a vague sense that the Holy Ghost was a "he." Most people never even think about it, let alone care. But as a *process*, it would seem to be very definitely feminine. For some Sophiologists, she might even have enclosed both God and Christ. What is important, I think, is that the question even arises. There is something called the "anamnesis of Sophia." It means the re-mem-

bering or regathering of those drops of light. Finding
her! So you have to follow the clues that she leaves so
obviously hidden that we overlook them.

Maybe, like all the rejected gods and goddesses of the
previous ages, Sophia had to hide out in fairy tales until some people came along and found her out, or she
touched them with her magic wand. Fairy tales have
proven to be a good hiding place for wisdom. They have
a way, like games, of hanging about from one generation to another.

I was rambling on when suddenly you turned with
eyes as big as saucers, as if you'd just been tapped yourself. "You don't mean..."

"Yes, I do, I really suspect it..."

"Are you suggesting that Sophia is the Fairy Godmother?"

"Ssshhh!" And then we laughed and looked right and
left, but we were safe on Iona. After all, it was the Celts
who worshipped Brid, a goddess of poetry, flocks, wisdom, and laughter. Theologians seem to forget the sense
and necessity for nonsense! Anyone without Sophia is
doomed to seriousness!

"But, seriously, how can you equate a Fairy Godmother with Hagia Sophia?" you asked.

Sophia has many disguises. It means starting, of
course, at the simplest, most childlike level. That's the
whole point. Sophia has humility, a word meaning

"close to the earth." She meets us at whatever level we are ready to meet her. And the Fairy Godmother is close, and comfy, and unthreatening. All children understand what she's about immediately. Sophia never insists, she has all eternity to wait in, and speaking purely gynecomorphically (how's that for a word!), I think there could be a twinkle in her eye as she waits for us to see the joke of it. Even Kali, the most frightening Great Mother in India, whose many arms hold up knives, skulls, and other scary things, has one hand up in blessing, as if to say, "Not to worry, follow me."

Stop and think. What are the characteristics of Fairy Godmothers? What does the name imply but Mother-of-God, the *theotokos*, the godbearer. She well could represent in a childlike way the very process within the psyche through which we might come to see with a loving eye. As Sophia, on a far more profound psychological level, she becomes inner mother to the Divine Child, the incarnating Self within us. It is through her, they say, that we are born again. As Meister Eckhart said: "All our souls are mothers to God," and he also said, "To grasp God in all things—that is the sign of your new birth." Sophia is an image, a most beautiful image, a personification of a most beautiful process. It is through her star-topped flowering wand, if you will, that we perceive those insights, those "ahas!" As Wisdom she is our constant inner teacher and guide.

At the child's level in us, then, we see that the Fairy Godmother in fairy tales is always helping and comforting would-be young heroes and heroines with down-to-earth *practical* advice: be kind to the wounded animal, share your sandwich with the hungry dwarf, watch out for this and for that. She is not a theologian addressing our minds; she addresses our hearts. I believe that down deep inside every one of us there is a sneaking hope that we have a "guardian angel" or that a Fairy Godmother truly exists. And she does! In the sense that what we are really talking about is an *archetype*, which we personify in different ways according to our level of understanding and our culture. Sophia has many, many disguises! But we can't go running about taking this out of context, please! It is a paradox, true symbolically rather than literally. They won't burn us at the stake, but there's always the funny farm!

I asked you to think about the Magic Wand. What does it have at the top?

"A star? Is that a hint towards the key of astrology?"

It sure was for me, because I learned that the planets rule archetypal processes that are universal, both in the world and in the psyche, and that that was why they were personified as gods and goddesses. For me they proved that the outer and the inner, and the inner and the outer, are One—the *unus mundus.*

The "fairy" part might hint that Sophia is at home in both realities (from our perception), and that her wand can make them one. According to Florensky, who wrote *La Sagesse de Dieu,* her motto is: *"Omnia coniungo" (I unite all things).* The archetypal image is really delightful, for the very reason that she hides in the least obvious places that you would ever look. Most people look down on fairy tales as just make-believe. But they all start with that big clue: "Once upon a time. . ."

"Then what does the wand symbolize?" you wanted to know.

For that, we would have to think of all the wands, staffs, rods, and their like that are hiding in other mythologies and cultures. Then see what they have in common, and if they are pointing in any way to one that you might have in your own body but are not fully aware of: the plant that grows in both our worlds that Jung spoke about in my dream.

Some people were wandering around with cameras and, hard as it was to interrupt our conversation, we decided to break for lunch and return to the lovely nunnery in the afternoon.

I started ahead of you and was waiting for you. I sat watching two puppies frisking and rolling about when you arrived almost out of breath. "Sorry I'm late, but I was talking to the lady at the desk. I told her what a magical spot Iona is, and do you know what? She said, 'We on Iona always feel that the veil between worlds is thinner here!' "

She's probably right! Anyway, you had brought Jung's *Answer to Job,* and I came with one of my favorite books, *Aurora Consurgens,* an alchemical work possibly written by Thomas Aquinas, which Dr. von Franz has edited and commented on.

You had some quotations of Jung's about Wisdom from the Bible to share. "Here, listen to this," you said:

"I am the mother of fair love, and fear, and knowledge, and holy hope: I therefore being eternal, am given to all my children which are chosen of him."

The pneumatic nature of Sophia as well as her world-building Maya character come out still more clearly in the apochryphal Wisdom of Solomon. "For Wisdom is a loving spirit," "kind to man." She is "the worker of all things," "in her is an understanding spirit, holy." She is "the breath of the power of God, a pure effluence flowing from the glory of the Almighty," "the brightness of the everlasting light, the unspotted mirror of the power of God," a being "most subtil," who "passeth and goeth through all things by reason of her pureness." She is "conversant with God," and "the Lord of all things himself loved her." "Who of all that are is a more cunning workman than she?" She is sent from heaven and from the throne of glory as a "Holy Spirit." As a psychopomp she leads the way to God and assures immortality.

Then it was my turn to share the words of Petrus Bonus, analchemist who lived in 1564 and had a great pen name! Dr. von Franz quotes him in a footnote in *Aurora Consurgens* as the author of the following:

. . . and this (the fixing and permanence of soul and spirit) cometh to pass through the addition of the secret stone which is not to be comprehended by the senses, but solely through understanding by divine inspiration or revelation or by the teaching of one that knoweth . . . and Alexander said:

There are two orders in this art, that is, beholding by the eye and understanding by the *heart* [italics mine], and this is the secret stone which is rightly called a gift of God, and is the divine, secret stone . . . and this divine stone is the heart and the tincture of the gold, which is sought by the philosophers.

So, they too sought to see with a loving eye. We got up in silence and by common consent walked again to

the jetty. The ferry was heading in. Men and boys were
busy with crates and boxes, some women and children
were waiting, the little ones jumping up and down in
their bright hand-knitted sweaters. The tide was low,
revealing more enchanting wet pebbles. The water fell
onto the sand with little weak slaps. It was a heavenly
turquoise color, the color of the Aegean, and also by
tradition, the color of Sophia. We went to the grocery
store and picked up a few things and dropped in at the
public lavatory. By then, the ferry was churning in and
clanging down the large metal front—a sound you could
hear all over the island—and the jetty came alive with
activity. Like the locals, we stood and watched folk
greeting and separating, with smiles and hugs or hand-
shakes. You seemed quite pensive.

Then, as we walked up the path once more you turned
to me and said: "I thought of another wand. 'Thou lead-
est me beside the still waters, thou restoreth my soul.
Yea, though I walk through the valley of the shadow
of death thou art with me, thy rod and thy staff, they
comfort me.' Do you suppose Hagia Sophia has something to do with the serpent power, the energy flow up
the spine—you know—the *kundalini*?"

I will never forget the wisdom in your smile.

*[By Gerhard Dorn, the alchemist]
we are told that it is Sophia, the Sa-
pientia, Scientia, or Philosophia
from whose fount the waters gush
forth. This Wisdom is the nous that
lies hidden and bound in matter, the
serpens mercurialis (the serpent of
Mercury)...*

C. G. Jung

*[The Holy Ghost] is the breath that
heals and makes whole...*

*[The Holy Ghost] is a function, but
that function is the Third Person of
the Godhead.*

*God will be begotten in creaturely
man...the future indwelling of the
Holy Ghost in man amounts to a
continuing incarnation of God.*

C. G. Jung

*Nous n'avons pas le choix: nous
devons nous enraciner dans l'amour,
âme véritable de la terre.*

*(We have no choice: we must root
ourselves in love, the veritable soul
of the earth.)*

Pierre Teilhard de Chardin

VII

Serpents

"Was Iona always such a spiritual focus?" was your next question. We had chosen to walk past the general store, heading southward this time. Your intuition already seemed to pick up a slight change in atmosphere. There are tales of people with second sight even "seeing" the terrible massacre of monks by the Vikings at Martyrs' Bay in 806 A.D., as if the slaughter had imprinted itself on the aura of the place. In fact, several times in succeeding centuries Iona was pillaged and the monks put to the sword.

The small strand we had reached was also supposed to be the landing spot for the funerary barges carrying the bodies of many Norwegian and Scottish kings and chieftains to their burial next to St. Oran's Chapel. Macbeth was one of them. This is where the *Straid nam Marbh*, the Road of the Dead, began, ending along those imposing stones that lead up to the present abbey. One cannot help but wonder at the reasoning behind such

89

a vicious attack on defenseless men. There is a theory
that it came as an outburst of Norse anger against a
forced conversion to Christianity by Charlemagne's
henchmen through betrayal and massacre—a very ugly
story. Indeed, you told me North German children grew
up calling Charlemagne the "butcher of Saxons."

We stood on the beach surveying some empty plastic
bottles washed ashore and caught in dead and black-
ened seaweed. Overhead, out of nowhere, two R.A.F.
fighters sliced low across the island in a deafening roar.
A cloud passed over the sun, and we shivered a little.
The shadow was here as well, and it brought to mind
the centuries that are basically unaccounted for on Iona,
when people lived in abject poverty in stone hovels, suffering the damp dark winters and dying of tuberculosis.
Even as late as 1793, when the island was visited by
Samuel Johnson and James Boswell, there was only one
house with a chimney. The rest had an opening in the
thatched roof for the smoke from the peat which burned
in the center of the house on the earthen floor. The people would not have supposed in their wildest dreams that
thousands upon thousands would someday come just to
set foot on their island. But the spirit of Columba never
left the place, and Johnson was to remark: "That man
is little to be envied, whose patriotism would not gain
force upon the plain of Marathon, or whose piety would
not grow warmer among the ruins of Iona."

We walked pensively southward and then turned west
along the road to the Hill of the Angels from which you
can look to another hill, *Sithean Mor*, the Fairy Mound.
According to Adamnan, Columba's first biographer,
Columba was seen praying on the former, surrounded

by flying angels. Here we separated spontaneously, you and I, agreeing to meet back on the road in two hours. I would climb the Fairy Mound and you, the Hill of the Angels.

I scrambled up and chose a small hollow filled with heather to spread my parka upon, and then sat down and surveyed the scene. A red and white cow and her calf were grazing serenely in the distance, and my attention was caught by a multitude of tiny yellow flowers here and there in the grass. Further down I could see the white puffs of bog cotton all bowing in the same direction as the wind passed over them. And I thought of Columba's prophecy:

> *In Iona of my heart, Iona of my love*
> *Where monks' voices were*
> *Shall be lowing of cattle*
> *But ere the world shall come to an end*
> *Iona will be as it was.*

Somehow, this day, my heart was heavy. Uninvited, a memory came up that seemed to epitomize an attitude in the world. I saw myself driving down the ramp to a parkway in Connecticut. Spring. Trees with the bright blues of periwinkle around their feet. Then suddenly the dead body of a discarded kitten in the middle of the road, killed as it had crept forward to eat from a discarded paper bag from somebody's lunch. It was a microcosmic image, given the human suffering in the world at large. But, as Winston Churchill remarked, "The death of one person is a tragedy, the death of a hundred, a statistic." With all the studies in cost efficiency, who has counted the hours, days, months, years of parenting and education which are snuffed out in a few seconds in violence and wars. How much of tragedy is pitiful waste!

I thought of His Holiness, the Dalai Lama, smiling and extending the strength of his two hands to us in Dharmsala, and his belief that the only true religion in the world is that of kindness. Compassion towards all sentient beings until every last one is returned whole to spirit. Patience, endurance, kindness—"Love suffereth long..." Why should it be so hard for so many simply to be kind? To hear a "new" commandment: Love thy neighbor, he *is* thyself! To know, not only believe, that the light of the Self in anyone else is the same light that is burning in the Self within us, so to reverence them both is to reverence the One, that great mystery of the Sacred.

How often, too, have we seen the scale tip the other way? We consciously feel guilty that we are not loving our neighbor enough and unconsciously constellate the opposite. It is as if, were we playing gin rummy, we were to deal the cards saying: One for you, and one for you, and one for you—oh, well, maybe one for me— and then we lose the game, having set ourselves up to lose in the name of mistaken "Christian" charity, a very subtle ego game. This in turn constellates deep hurt and even anger in the unconscious. We did not hear the words "Love thy neighbor *as thyself*." We heard "as thy ego," which must be bad. Sometimes, if one cannot give oneself a fair deal, it helps to rephrase the statement as, "One for you and one for my Divine Guest," if only to set up the relationship fairly and not make the other person feel obligated. Balance.

We in the West are out of balance in our symbolic thinking. We banished Sophia from the Holy Trinity, leaving only her token, the dove. The divine triad of power gradually became entirely masculine, leaving the divinity of the receptive and creative feminine process outside of it. What would this say through the centuries to men and to women alike? As Jung has pointed out, both woman and shadow (the devil) became the hidden fourth, and it wasn't long before the two were blended, and we unconsciously projected evil onto witches accused of consorting with Satan. This projection was acted out throughout the Middle Ages with thousands of women, with the men who protested it, going to fiery deaths at the stake, branded as heretics by Inquisitors ignorant of the fact that in so doing the fiend was walking through the backdoor of their own psyches.

This forgetting of Sophia has cost humanity dearly. Without her a sword seems to separate men and women, and a struggle for supremacy is underway on the part of both. A separation that only the greatest love and mutual appreciation can overcome. It is as if Sophia stepped into a tree and hid from us. I smiled at that image, since the words "tree," "truth," and "Druid" are said to be cognate.

The blaming of woman is certainly mirrored in the story of Adam and Eve. Both the serpent and Eve are seen as tempting poor Adam into consciousness, obviously a necessary evolution for humanity, yet to this day seen as a sin and a "Fall." In psychological terms, the story suggests tht Eve conceived the ego (the center of consciousness) by the serpent, just as Mary conceived the Christ-Self through the dove. Symbolically speaking, there seems to be a relationship between the serpent and the dove, and both are connected to Sophia, as we shall see. We cannot acquire wisdom without consciousness, and yet we have to sacrifice our identification with ego consciousness before we can approach a loving and devoted relationship to the scintilla of spirit within us called the Self. But wisdom does not live in the ego, it lives in the soul, in the heart rather than the mind. This Holy Wisdom is loving as well as wise. If you look at the symbol of the caduceus, it is surmounted by wings.

So to be "wise as a serpent and harmless as a dove" takes on a deeper meaning. (The word "harmless" is variously translated as "pure," "simple," and "meek" in different versions of the Gospel of Matthew, (10:16). The word "simple," *einfaltig* as it appears in German, meaning whole, might be a better version.) Sophia is "loving and kind towards men."

The Tree of the Knowledge of Good and Evil, if you come to think of it, has one serpent. Together Eve and that serpent have carried the blame for turning this Tree of Knowledge into a Tree of Death. But the Tree of Life has two serpents, and perhaps to understand this better we need to look to the East or to reexamine the secret and concealed images of the rejected mystics and alchemists of the West. In the myth, Adam and Eve are cast out lest they stretch forth their hands and take of the fruit of the Tree of Life and become as the gods. And yet Jesus told his disciples: "Ye are gods."

Way off in the distance, a fishing boat was making its way through the silver sea. It was a lovely sight. I scrunched deeper into my heather bed and went on free-associating. One serpent led us into this world of duality and ego consciousness, but two serpents, balanced, as on the caduceus of the spinal staff, might unite two into a reborn One. Here myths and images would converge if we could with Sophia's help decode their meaning.

Next I saw again the *phiale,* a huge stone lavabo at Hagia Sophia, the immense sixth-century domed church built by the Emperor Justinian from 532-537 A.D. in what was formerly Constantinople. It was later converted to a Moslem mosque and today it is a museum in Istanbul. It, too, has two enormous serpents sculpted on it, and my thoughts were to come back to it.

But for now I stretched out in the heather and looked up at the sky, suddenly remembering my first experience of that place. I was five and a half years old. My father had been sent to Turkey to oversee the distribution of linotype machines to all the Turkish newspapers which were converting from the Arabic to the Roman alphabet at the state decree of Ataturk. We spent a month on the idyllic island of Prinkipo in the Sea of Marmara, from which my father could commute to the city by a small day boat.

On this particular day, Nanny had apparently been given the day off, so my parents included me on an excursion to Istanbul. I remember the boat trip, the dark shy eyes of the other children, and the Island of Dogs, where stray dogs were supposedly left to starve to death. When we got to the city my father and mother decided to go to the Great Bazaar.

This place has to be seen to be believed! (Even after fifty years the memories, sounds, and smells had not changed, they had only intensified.) The Great Bazaar is a covered arcade with hundreds of small shops, lined up side by side in a bewildering labyrinth of corridors which are lit by serpentine strings of light bulbs. Here silversmiths, leatherworkers, carpet sellers, food merchants, strolling peddlers, jewelers, and toy venders are still to be found, cheek by jowl. At the entrances sat men smoking hookah pipes or telling their holy beads through rough fingers. The delicious smell of coffee, the sweet smell of confections and rose-flavored Turkish Delight permeated the air. I remember my parents discussing their plans over my head, each to do something different, and agreeing to meet later. While they were talking, I could not resist slipping around the corner to look in yet another shop, confident that they saw me. The upshot was each parted quite certain that I was safely with the other parent. This was not the case.

I sped from shop to shop, turning corners, feasting on sights for several minutes before, to my horror, I realized there was no familiar face behind me. Then I ran and ran, up and down the alleys, panic settling in. Finally I came to a stop in front of a rug seller and burst into tears.

He had a white beard and a sort of turban on his head. To my surprise and relief he spoke to me in English. "You are lost, my child, are you not?" I nodded. "Then come here and let's see if we can help you. What is your name? How old are you?" At each response I made, he beamed praise and reassurance. He led me into his tiny shop which was filled with the most beautiful richly colored rugs and carpets. "Tell me now, which is your favorite one? Why is this your favorite?"

Gently he directed me to the pattern in the carpet. "Supposing, little Alice, you were a fly walking on this carpet. What color would you think the world was if you were here?" "Blue," I said. "And here?" "Green." "And look at this big stretch!" "Red, dark red." I was calming down. "If you were that fly wouldn't you feel mixed up? First this, then that, then that and this, and that and this again?" He said it very fast so I laughed. It must have been a good description of my own impression of life. "Now, do you know what a design is?" I nodded. "Tell me, what can the little fly do to make sense of all those different colors?" I thought hard, and he gave me a big hint. "What can it do that you cannot yet? Think what it is called. . . ." "Fly!" I fairly shouted. "Right! Then he can see the design from another level. It makes sense then, doesn't it?" He caressed my cheek and said to me, "Do you think you can remember that?" I promised I would. Then he took me by the hand, asked a neighboring shopkeeper to mind his shop, and led me out of the mysterious bazaar into the crowded sunlit street. In the middle of the road stood a policeman directing traffic. As the two men spoke rapidly in Turkish to one another, I could see the deference accorded my guide by the law officer. He bowed repeatedly and with the greatest respect. Within a minute, I saw my mother on the sidewalk screaming over the traffic. "There she is!" I cried.

I expected a spanking right then and there, but no, it was a tearful reunion. Years later, my mother told me that she was going to offer the man a reward, but he must have read her thoughts. With a kind flick of the eye, it seems, he forestalled her and, placing his hand over his heart, he bowed to Mother and then with a tender smile to me. I didn't want to leave him!

After lunch, we went to Hagia Sophia, now a museum. There we took off our shoes and were given paper slippers. These were so big that I ended up sort of skiing through the enormous, vaulted, beautiful serenity of the place. It was even bigger than any railroad station, really big enough for God!

Fifty-three years later, with you safely holding my hand, I walked again through the Great Bazaar and these memories welled up in me. On this day, I had been given leave from the Chi-ops group in order to seek out Sheikh Muzaffer Ozak of the al Jerrahi al Halveti Order of Dervishes, God's Mercy upon him, a Sufi master in a centuries-old succession. We were accompanied by James Fadiman, who already knew him, and he in-

structed us on how to behave when we got to his bookstore. (All Sufis work in the world.)

Jim's eyes lit up in anticipation. "When he comes in,
since he does not speak English, he will get a feeling
about you. Then he may offer you a cigarette. Take it
even if you do not smoke. If he lights it and touches your
hand, you will have received *baraka,* the transmission
of Spirit. It is a great blessing," said Jim.

We arrived at the small bookstore, which consisted
of two rooms. Chairs were lined up in the room on the
right, and various people were sitting there quietly. In
the room to the left was a huge desk covered with a confusion of papers, with four chairs lined up against the
wall to the right of it. We were greeted by a man with
glowing eyes, a man radiating sweetness, who introduced himself as Ibrahim. He directed us to the chairs.
He too bowed with his hand over his heart. He spoke
English and told us that the Efendi would soon arrive.
In my mind's eye I fully expected my friend, the white-
bearded rug seller. In the meantime, we bought a good
translation of the Koran.

Shortly thereafter, in walked Sheikh Muzaffer. He
was a big, vigorous, handsome man with prominent eye-
brows and a moustache, and he was dressed in grey
slacks and a bright yellow, v-necked sweater. He sat
down at his desk, exuding life and good humor. I sat
stunned because his face so resembled that of M, my
teacher, it was like seeing him in the flesh again. The
Sheikh's eyes were merry and every time he sneaked a
peek at me, they imparted a sense of sharing some delightful secret. He looked at you, and then at me, and

back at you, as if he knew that we belonged together. He greeted Jim most fondly and sent for some coffee. The room filled with energy and joy. Out came the cigarettes, and he lit each of ours, actually touching our hands as he did so. Through Ibrahim we chatted about small matters. His merriment increased. He called for gifts. An exquisitely hand-calligraphed page of the Holy Koran for my meditation room; a beautiful *Bismillah* (the name of Allah) inscribed in the shape of a peacock for you. We received his autographed picture with blessings on the back. The bookstore almost levitated into another realm. A young man from afar arrived in a business suit. He leaned over the desk and greeted the Sheikh, and we saw the love, the respect, the utter devotion of disciple and master. Power, majesty, love and bliss filled the shop. It was hard, so very hard to leave! But we rose and said good-bye and walked out onto the little stone courtyard. All of a sudden there was a huge shout, a roar behind us. There stood the Efendi blowing kisses, thrusting out his great hands to send them to us. We waved and blew them back. So overwhelming was the experience that instead of shopping for any souvenirs, we made our way to the Blue Mosque, there to sit quietly in another soaring holy space to gather it all in.

Nor was that quite all. Jim decided to walk back to the ship, and you and I took a taxi. When we got to the dock, I went in, leaving you to pay the driver. This took so long that I went out again to find you. You were standing with a man who wanted to exchange a torn dollar bill for a whole one. You did not have one, so I looked in my purse and gave the man one. Then the man looked up and said: "Lady, wait! Please wait!" We watched him rush up the sidewalk to a flower vendor. There he grabbed a bunch of beautiful red roses and ran back. "Lady," he said. "For you, for free, for you." He gave us the roses and bowed with a smile holding his hand over his heart. With a shock, I remembered M and the time we had talked together alone in the presence of a single rosebud on the mantlepiece. I was twenty-one and he in his seventies. By the end of the conversation, the rose had opened. He led me up to it and asked me to look at it. "Dearie, always remember that you have watched and seen a rose open." It is the special flower of Sophia.

All these memories condensing from far away on a hill on Iona! But I had been thinking of the stone font at Hagia Sophia, had I not? When we went there the first time, I had discovered, hidden away in a back room, this enormous vessel made of a single block of stone, and I was eager and excited to show it to you. There it still was in the back room.

It has two serpents opposed in bas-relief winding out of it, which free their heads completely both to drink out of and to inform the holy waters within. The sculptor would have had to free them from the stone block itself while chiseling, no mean feat! Yet, how symbolically appropriate to Sophia! Through the twin serpents, the spirit of Holy Wisdom is released from the stone. I later found out from the director that such phiales go back to the reign of the Byzantine Basil I (867-886) and were used for washing the eyes and hands. Were we to wash our eyes in the waters of wisdom today, perhaps our vision of reality might change.

The phiale in Hagia Sophia

Another symbolic font, of course, is the baptismal one, which implies that through baptism—of the transformative kind given by John the Baptist to Jesus—we can hope for rebirth. And classically the dove is depicted both at the Annunciation and at that baptism in the Jordan. Christians claim these mysteries as their own, but surely they are to be shared as openly as Judaism has been shared through the Old Testament, or the Eastern religions have shared their wisdom with us. For it is time to see that all of these are expressions of universal mysteries, true for all humankind, because they describe "the only way" that Christ and Krishna spoke of as leading to the Father—surely the *process* necessary for human beings to fulfill the great task of individuation, which Jung equated theologically with incarnation.

That stone phiale in Istanbul looks like a grail. It is a holy vessel. So another clue came to mind: in the story of Parsifal, it is written that the dove renews the Grail once a year. So perhaps the Grail is Sophia's cup, the feminine vessel of the all-containing manifest world. It is her loving wisdom that sustains it. "Omnia coniungo," she whispers. I grinned a little, because I almost saw it written "Omnia con-Jung-o!" After all, much of this is the hidden import of Jung's *Mysterium Coniunctionis,* and the Philosopher's Stone: the necessity to yoke (yoga!) the opposites of dualities rather than to choose one side over the other, to hold on to both of them consciously and heal the splits apparent in the world within our own individual psyches, no matter how deep or how awful the pain of it. This is the nature of the Opus, the Work. Only in this way can we hope to love and heal our world: through working on our own stuff.

My thoughts were making me fairly intense, and I had
a fantasy of how wonderful it would be if a new dogma
honoring Sophia could be proclaimed, not by a Papal
Bull, but by a Papal Cow! I smiled at my own heretical
impiety, but felt comforted at the same time that one
of the secrets of Sophia is laughter. If one of the two
serpents is sense, then the other has to be nonsense! Besides, Sophia would protest any dogma whatsoever. One
of her other names is Dame Kinde, which means natural.
"Who can tell where the wind listeth?" A warm breeze
was blowing, and I thought I heard Sophia saying: "The
winds are my scarves."

I decided on a cup of tea, opened my rucksack, took
out the thermos, and poured some tea into the plastic
top. Not a very fancy teacup, but a container nevertheless, and as purposeful in its way as the baptismal font
is. Both share that same capacity of filling, containing,
and pouring forth anew, as would a womb or the Holy
Grail.

The Grail, in turn, made me think of Aquarius, the
Water Bearer. Except that Aquarius is not a water sign,
it is an air sign, and those zig-zags pouring out of his
vessel are not water but represent invisible energy,
prana, and so, if you think of it, the glyph of Aquarius
♒ can be seen to be two serpents, perhaps the two
serpents representing the *ida* and *pingala*, invisible
energy currents that we all carry in our own subtle
bodies. So, if the New Age of Aquarius is Joachim's Age
of the Holy Spirit, then it will be the Age of Sophia as
well, which will perhaps herald the evolutionary opening of the "third eye," the loving eye, within the next

two thousand years. Perhaps the vessel Aquarius carries is truly none other than Sophia's cup, the treasured
mystical Grail that held the wine of Christ-consciousness, the pure spirit of love, shed for us all, whoever we
are, so long as we are humble and ecumenical enough
to receive it in the spirit it was given, to circulate it as
mystical blood, and share it with joy and gratitude.

The sun was lowering like a wafer into the cup of the
ocean—Teilhard de Chardin's beautiful image. I got up
hastily and put on my parka. Two hours had sped by
out of time and space. I felt "repumpitated" now and
was curious to know how you had fared on the Hill of
the Angels. I looked for you and saw that you, too, were
looking for me. We both waved our cromags, our Scottish sticks, and I felt welling up inside me wonder that
you had come into my life. Dear Muzaffer, a blessing
upon his memory, must have seen it.

When we met, and after hugs, you handed me a tiny
posy made of those diminutive flowers that grow on
Iona. "These were the biggest flowers I could find," you
said, "but they do come from the Hill of the Angels."
I looked at them and laughed, for Sophia's face was shining up out of each of them.

DAWN ON IONA

Listen—
Sea-raptures, dappling of waves,
Wet shadows, dark-leaping light.
High on Mull, silver-singing burns
Are streaming light.
Heather bending,
Sheep bedewed and wind-carved crosses,
Rock. O black and dreaming mountains!
Shimmering mosses.

Look—
A counter-point of gulls
Stitching white screams
Random on the harbours
Awake from grey and tidal dreams
There—glory leaping
Up the purple-misted bay
To fling this sudden dazzling silence
Across a Hebridean day.

A.O

THE MYSTERY

I am the wind which breathes upon the sea,
I am the wave of the ocean,
I am the murmur of the billows,
I am the ox of the seven combats,
I am the vulture upon the rocks,
I am a beam of the sun,
I am the fairest of plants
I am a wild boar in valour,
I am a salmon in the water,
I am a lake in the plain,
I am a word of science
I am the point of the lance of battle,

I am the god who created in the head the fire
Who is it who throws light into the meeting on the
    mountain?
Who announces the ages of the moon?
Who teaches the place where couches the sun?
  (If not I)

From the Leabhar Gabala Eirann,
Tr. by Douglas Hyde

VIII

Flowers

We strolled back on the road, hand in hand, at a lei-
surely pace. We could have clambered the shortcut over
the moor, but since the road was empty and glistening
in the late afternoon's slanting light, walking it became
a pleasure in itself. There was nothing to hurry for or
to. There are no "entertainments" on Iona, no cinema,
no lecture hall, no traffic, and though there is a golf
course of sorts on the machair, in all the times that I
have now been on Iona, I have never seen any golf
players other than a few reflective, cud-chewing cows.
No, Iona offers the visitor only a choice of worship: out-
doors in its holiness, or within its human precincts: the
beautiful abbey, St. Oran's Chapel, the Bishop's House,
or the Parish Church. The bustling activity of the young
folk of the Iona Community is centered and clustered
close about the abbey itself: the choir, the classes, and
now the building of the Macleod Center. There is a
beautiful spirit to the work they do, and one sees it in
their faces, but they seem naturally somewhat closed off
from the transient visitors at the two hotels on the island.
As we were to discover, our hotel, St. Columba's Hotel,
was the occasional meeting place for what one of my

daughters has labeled the "lama-lama" people, or New
Age groups. These consist of groups of twenty to thirty
people with guides, coming to Iona from afar to visit,
meditate, and study among themselves. There is also a
small Findhorn colony at the north of the island. Twice
a week the island breathes in the hundreds of boat pilgrims who spend about three hours exploring the abbey and the few craft shops and museum. Yet, peace
and quiet abound.

You began to share your thoughts gathered on the Hill
of Angels. "One of the comforting things about Sophia,
as I understand her, is that she is there for anybody."
You said that one does not have to be a theologian, or
a scholar, or even have to read hundreds of books to
understand her. "You know that I never had time to
read. I always was so busy working all my life. Then
the war, and then caring for my family, and for my dear
wife who fought cancer for ten years—I simply could
not study the way you did." And yet you knew, you understood something about Sophia. "In a way, it seems
to me that she is playing a game with us, but no one
has ever explained the rules of the game! For me, that
makes it difficult."

Then you went on to say that being a man, you like
to organize your thinking in such a way that at least you
could learn to think in another way. And you laughed.
"The way I see it, Wisdom is hiding everywhere, but
we haven't learned how to *look*, so that makes it very
hard to see. It's a bit like those puzzles for children I
remember, where you had to count how many animals
you could find hidden in the picture of a tree, or how

The village street

many words you could find concealed within other words or where they joined together. It's certainly not the way most of us are educated to look."

Then I tried to explain that the mystics have been saying that the sacred is very well hidden in the commonplace, and that the way to unlock the wisdom in this world is to learn to think and live symbolically. To do that, they say, you have to find the process hidden in everyday manifestations about us in nature and even in ordinary objects, because there can be nothing in this manifest world outside of the universal processes that govern their existence.

So Sophia holds the key, and we have to find it. Thus the rules of the game involve following certain clues. These are hidden in:

(a) nature
(b) the religions of the world (esoterically understood)
(c) sacred geometry
(d) myths and fairy tales
(e) archetypal processes in and outside the psyche
(f) astrology and alchemy
(g) the human body
(h) dreams
(i) words (etymology)

If you showed it as a petaled flower, it would look like this. And each petal could lead you to the center.

"So, it's a matter of finding the key." You stopped to watch a bird flying high across the island. Maybe it was a golden eagle, but you weren't sure. "Wasn't there a Mullah story about a key?" you asked.

"You mean Mullah Nasruddin, the eleventh-century idiot sage of the Sufis?"

You knew a tale about him I had never heard so, much to your delight, you shared it. "Well, one day a friend found Mullah hunting for something outside his house. He was poking under bushes and stones, when the friend queried: 'Hey, Mullah, what have you lost?'

'I've lost my keys!' cried Mullah.

Kindly the friend joined in what soon proved to be a fruitless scrabbling. 'Can't you remember at all where you lost them?'

Mullah looked up. 'Sure,' he said, 'I know exactly where I lost them. I lost them in the house.'

'Then, why on earth are you looking for them out here?'

'I can see better—it's so much lighter out here!' "

Don't we all do that—look around outside for the key we have lost inside us?

By then we had reached the hotel and were interrupted by the pleasure of a nice salmon supper and a good white wine. There were many-petaled little flowers on our table, each having the face of a little Sophia. We toasted her and each other and ate our supper eagerly and gratefully.

It was not until later, when we were lying in bed, looking out the window at Orion blazing in the night sky, that we resumed our conversation.

"So, what do you think the key is?" you asked.

"Well, for me, at least, it means matching images with meaning. *Omnia coniungo* must mean putting those two together. Most of education stresses meaning and leaves out the image, or else we just look at the images outside and inside us, and shake our heads because they have no meaning."

You explained that experience for you is like a video, an ongoing succession of images. "I mean, I have looked at trees all my life, but I, you know, I never really connected them to a meaning within me until you told me about M's exercise. But since then, I realize that if I looked at an image or a picture of a river and its feeding streams and brooks, or the veins in a leaf, or a lightning flash, or my own blood vessels, or nervous system, or the road system on a map, they would all have something in common—the same pattern, the same process. It seems so very obvious, but I never gave it a meaning.

I even can see that the structure of an outline for a school composition follows the same idea. The meaning might be discovering that the same process links these things, so that they resonate on different levels. That this branching from big to little might even work in ordering my own being. It made me think of the words in the Bible: "I am the vine and ye are the branches." In fact, I can see all kinds of meanings, like 'As above, so below.' Or as below, so above. Same difference."

"What about words and etymology?" I wanted to know. "I bet Sophia hides a lot there, too, and she probably pops up in the unconscious expressions we use. Even the word 'image' suggests a relationship to 'magic' and 'imagination,' because I can see a Magi hidden in the word, even though they may not come from the same root." [They don't, but the Magi is in there anyway!]

"I think Sophia likes puns, too," you agreed. "If you think about it, every time we imagine something, we are creating or co-creating, and we can associate that with something godlike. Just having that power in our mind is a wonder past belief, but I guess we mostly take it for granted."

"What I can't help marveling at is all the images that come in dreams so spontaneously from the unconscious but which, if you analyze them, often have profound meaning, symbolic meaning. In our dreams can be cities with all the buildings, shops with all the stuff in the windows, and there is space without space and time without time, of another dimension. How do we do it?"

"In German, you know," you said, "there is an expression *ein Sinnbild*. The *Sinn* means 'meaning' and the *bild* means 'picture.' Together the word translates as symbol. And that in Greek is *sym-bolon*, and I know that means to throw or join together, just like Sophia's *omnia coniungo*. Well, that's as far as I have gotten today," and you gave a big yawn. "But I think the first rule of the game is to play it, and the second is to play hide-and-seek with her, and the third is to put two and two together just like us!"

And you rolled over and gave me a hug and a goodnight kiss.

I lay awake a little longer, looking out the window and remembering a poem.

$$+ O + R + I + O + N +$$

Hazeltwig man
dowser of dawn
your stars are dipping
over my breast

* * *

and in my dream
the waters rise crystal
like early morning
when love is best.

That night Iona gave me the following dream, which I told you at breakfast:

I am in an octagonal library. The carpeted center holds the librarian and all the index cards. Each of the eight sides has a glass wall and a door. Above each section is carved a word. I see that LAW is over one. I choose the one with TRUTH over the lintel. Inside each of these sections there is a table and chairs, and the walls are lined with a marvelous collection of antique books, scrolls, and manuscripts. The bibliophile in me begins to hunger and thirst with excitement! But then I notice another door at the back of the room which leads into darkness, so I look through it and see a stairway leading down. I cannot resist descending the stairs which end in a cryptlike basement of cobbled stones. Windows let in a soft light and the rays of this light fall upon bunches and bunches of flowers and potted plants all in full bloom. The air is full of fragrance.

Since according to tradition Sophia is associated particularly with flowers, we began to play her game with the dream. Certainly, it seemed to suggest that a deeper truth is to be found in flowers than even in books!

Then you suggested that each of the natural kingdoms—mineral, vegetable and animal—seems to have a flowering, and among the flowers, one special one onto which we have collectively projected a special value.

The "flowers" of the mineral kingdom are jewels; the most symbolically precious being the diamond. It is the hardest natural substance on earth, and when mined and polished by humans, the most brilliant in reflecting light. The Sanskrit mantra: *Om mane padme om,* "the diamond is in the lotus," hints that the goal of incarnation would be the totality of body, psyche and spirit necessary to reflect God. This is what Jung called individuation, the teleology of every human psyche.

The vegetable kingdom blooms in its flowers, and the two most symbolic flowers are the lotus in the East and the rose in the West. Both are feminine symbols. The lotus is mystical because its roots are in the earth, it grows in water and opens its petals in air to the fire of the sun, thus combining the four basic elements. The rose, both the red and the white, is unique because it is grafted by a "gardener" onto a wild rosebush. A higher and a lower have been brought together through the agency of a still higher order or kingdom, namely the gardener. Both the diamond and the rose, therefore, are sublimated through human, by extension, spiritual intervention. So the symbolism behind the Rose and the Cross, as in Rosicrucianism, becomes rich in interpretations.

In both the lotus and the rose, as well as in other flowers, geometric symmetry, color, and fragrance yield more insights. The interdependence with bees, another "level," and the nectar of honey add more. I put in that I had attended a lecture by Rachel Fletcher, the geometer, which was spent almost entirely on the intricate geometry of an iris, connecting its proportions to those found in Greek architecture!

The "flowers" of the animal kingdom could be said to be human beings, if only because we carry within us the buds of Christ-consciousness. Collectively, we are far from blooming, though perhaps we see in the history of the great incarnate souls, our teachers and saviors, what might lie in store for us, if we would be willing to grow. (I could have said Bodhi- or Krishna-consciousness. This consciousness is open to souls of every faith, not the prerogative of only one. We need so desperately to honor and benefit from each other's religions, not to use them as weapons of separation!)

I mentioned that for me there is a certain danger in thinking hierarchically. As if the diamond were superior

to the stone or the rose to the potato. Or a Bodhisattva
to a nincompoop. Hierarchies belong to levels. Sometimes, it is the ego that ranks them and gives them im-
portance through pride. The rose cannot bloom without
roots in the dark earth. Nor can we as human beings
advance to higher consciousness without our humblest
beginnings. "Every saint was once a sinner." The higher
level depends upon the lower, and the spirit, like our
blood, *circulates,* joining the root to the blossom and
the blossom to the root.

Since the mystics teach that all the universe is con-
tained within the human body, we can ask about the
flowers within us and what they might symbolize.

This is where the kundalini might come in, because
the chakra centers in the subtle body are often depicted
as flowers or flowering wheels. It is a beautiful image
and carries with it the message of seeing the unfolding
of our consciousness through different levels as a *natural* process, never something to be forced. Such matters have to do with grace and with trusting the process.
Our task is simply to remove as many obstacles to the
natural flow of progress as possible.

The connection between Holy Wisdom (Sophia) and
the Holy Ghost remains the symbol of the dove, that
image with a meaning of love and of peace. Whether
carrying the olive branch on Christmas cards or flut-
tering on Valentine cards, doves keep appearing year
after year. But the deep symbolism is associated with
Pentecost, when the disciples gathered in the upper room
and the "flames" of the Holy Spirit opened up their
chakras, one could say, and they spoke in many tongues.

From what we know of the relationship of the process of kundalini today, it really would seem that the disciples experienced an opening of the higher chakras in a burst of cosmic consciousness, which resulted in their being given the ability to speak in other languages, among other things.

A powerful and monitory work on kundalini has been written by Gopi Krishna. In it he tells of his firsthand experiences with it, and of his agonies over many years when, through overstimulating the energy by breathing exercises, etc., his kundalini erupted. In the end, he, too, began to write and speak in languages he knew not that he knew.

Those who can read auras explain that the effect of total enlightenment or cosmic consciousness produces a nimbus of light around the body and a halo around the head. The saints are depicted like this, and in the East images of Buddha and the Bodhisattvas have protuberances on top of their heads. A careful study of native art all over the world will show attention drawn to the top of the head. The crown chakra is called the thousand-petaled lotus.

So the process of Sophia or the Holy Spirit, the Comforter or Paraclete, promised us by Christ must surely hint at kundalini, for it is through its flowering staff that we discover that "only way." It is a *method* (a technique rather than an exclusive road, a verb rather than a noun) enabling a Second Coming or our own rebirth within. This seems to me so vitally important to grasp. It could unite East and West in mutual understanding. Here, the dove present at the Annunciation to Mary connects with the necessary presence of Sophia's *process* for the rebirth of the Christ Within (or Atman). For we are told that the "Kingdom of Heaven is within" and that we can only enter it as little children. The paradox seems to suggest that rebirth is not an achievement so much as a surrender allowing love and wisdom to unite within us. It is much easier for the ego to insist than to allow. So when we learn to think with our hearts and love with our minds, an important *coniunctio* has taken place within. It is all made to sound so very complicated and scary, but I strongly suspect that the method itself is very simple, and that only by simplifying can we hope to make progress.

Well, what about the books in the dream? I asked myself. "Books [one of my passions!]," said my teacher, "only help to mirror what you know already. You simply read who you are and the rest spills over while your mind turns to cement! But they are very good for learning vocabularies with which to talk to other people. Sophia will talk gastronomy with the cook, and electricity with the electrician, so to speak. They give you knowledge, but you have to turn that into wisdom through living it."

You can read all about kundalini nowadays, and one should know about it and its risks. Certainly one of the greatest areas of confusion, because of ignorance on the part of the practitioners, is the connection between spiritual ambition and sex. How many Eastern and Western gurus have we read of recently who have fallen by the wayside through confusing the two! The rush of energy gets concentrated in the lower chakras, and women are used instead of loved. So if the "serpent power" is awakened without the presence of the dove, things can go mightily askew.

Better to start with the Fairy Godmother, who will always give you exactly as much as you need to know when you need to know it. Personally, I always remember in the fairy tale of "Mother Holle" what happened to the ambitious stepsister who tried to get the shower of gold without doing the legwork, and who ended up with a shower of pitch instead.

All of the above emerged as we interspersed various activities on Iona with thoughtful conversations. We began to think each other's thoughts so often, that in the end we decided we must be half-wits!

"But I forgot to mention one last thing. How do you know when you are playing the game with Sophia right?" you asked as you rolled up your napkin neatly and pushed it into the napkin ring.

"Maybe, it's when synchronicities occur. It must be her way of winking!"

KINSHIP

I am aware,
As I go commonly sweeping the stair;
Doing my part of the every-day care—
Human and simple my lot and share—
I am aware of a marvelous thing:
Voices that murmur and ethers that ring
In the far stellar spaces where cherububims sing;
I am aware of the passion that pours
Down the channels of fire through Infinity's doors;
Forces terrific, with melody shod,
Music that mates with the pulses of God,
I am aware of the glory that runs
From the core of myself to the core of the suns,
Bound to the stars by invisible chains,
Blaze of eternity now in my veins,
Seeing the rush of ethereal rains,
Here in the midst of the every-day air—
I am aware.

I am aware
As I sit quietly here in my chair,
Sewing or reading or braiding my hair—
Human and simple my lot and my share—
I am aware of the systems that swing
Through the aisles of creation on heavenly wing,
I am aware of a marvelous thing,
Trail of the comets in furious flight
Thunders of beauty that shatter the night,
Terrible triumph of pageants that march
To the trumpets of time of Eternity's arch.
I am aware of the splendour that ties
All the things of the earth with the things of the skies,
Here in my body the heavenly heat,
Here in my flesh the melodious beat
Of the planets that circle Divinity's feet.
As I silently sit here in my chair,
I am aware.

Angela Morgan

IX
a day of Joy

The bell of the abbey proclaimed that it was Sunday, so we joined the streams of figures being pulled into the church from various directions, and chose two of the wooden chairs near the aisle so that we could see down the length of the nave to the sunlit altar. To our left were the successive romanesque arches of a doorway from the original ruins of the abbey. It was small, and quite the coziest part of the church. The choir stalls were filling with young people, who shortly burst into song. The service was conducted by both a minister and his wife in cheerful and thick Glaswegian accents. I loved the sound of every word. The spirit was strong and positive, the music stirring, and the sermon, as I remember, touched with realism and humor.

Afterwards we walked again through the cloister and admired the bronze sculpture by Jacques Lipschitz of a dove topping a womblike flower. It is called "Descent of the Spirit."

We left the abbey and stepped out into yet another glorious day. There the living white doves were ascend-

The abbey of Iona

ing, flying and swooping about a small sunken garden. We stopped at the coffee shop to pick up a picnic lunch and then headed due north to the White Strand of the Monks at the top of the island. Here the sands were clear and clean, and the lovely turquoise and sapphire waters inviting, though cold. No one was about. We slipped off our boots and socks and waded, picked up more pebbles, and wrote love notes to each other in the hard sand, knowing the sea would sweep them into its billowing unconscious to save them for the ages, perhaps to roll them back to us on some future shore in some future life. Your cheeks were as rosy as your feet, and so, I guess, were mine. We laughed and played like children, since we were alone and unself-conscious. Then we scrambled to a hollow in the dunes and sat with the rough tall grasses at our back, secure in the sunlight and hungry for sandwiches. And we talked about poetry and we talked about books, and living firsthand and second hand.

"We are all like two little birds in a tree," said Ramakrishna. "One of them eats the fruit and the other one watches."

I tried to defend my years and years of practicing the *lectura divina*, the daily search through reading for spiritual growth. According to our temperaments, yoga has been sorted into four main strands or practices: karma yoga, the way of action, in which one dedicates all the fruits of one's actions to God; bhakti yoga, the path of love, worship, and devotion; jnana yoga, the path of knowledge; and raja yoga, the royal path of total dedication, the way of the monastic. But all could lead one in the end to enlightenment. You opted enthusiastically for karma yoga, and I still wasn't quite sure where I was, even after fifty years of study! Teasingly, you challenged me, and asked me when my reading had ever had a dramatic effect on my life. The question actually made me giggle, because it brought up a hilarious memory.

I was nineteen and had been living in New York at Evangeline House, a Salvation Army residential hotel for young women. The hostess there was a Canadian woman, and she invited me to spend the summer on her family's farm in Manitoba. It was wartime, and they were short-handed, so I could earn my keep. As you know, I agreed to go. So, duly I found myself en route to Montreal, where I had to change trains for one crossing the continent.

The journey was an overnight one. I remember I had dressed my smartest with high heels and even a boxy fur jacket to top things off. I settled my things and sat down to read my current *lectura divina*, which happened to be by St. Augustine. I was feeling very grown-up and independent.

Shortly after the train began to move, I thought it might be exciting to try the club car. So, I made my way there and sat down, to be joined almost immediately by a most distinguished-looking Royal Canadian Air Force officer, who sat down beside me. He had pink cheeks and white hair at the temples. He was most friendly and offered to buy me a sherry. We were on our second when the club car attendant announced that the bar was closed, but that we could take our drinks back to our seats.

"Jolly good!" cried the colonel. "Let's do!" So we tottered (at least I did in my heels) back to my seat only to discover that all the seats had been made up into berths and were now hung with long green curtains. It was obviously getting late. I wasn't too sure of etiquette under these circumstances, so I sat primly on the edge of my berth, and the colonel sat beside me, forcing people to climb over our legs as they went up and down the aisle. It wasn't long before the colonel suggested that we "pop in" for the sake of convenience.

So, in we popped. He sat cross-legged at one end of the bed and I at the other, drinks in hand. The train rocketed through the night; distant lights flashed dimly across our faces in the dark intimacy of the berth. The colonel was beginning to warm to the occasion, and before I knew it, he had moved very close to me, his arm was around me, and his hands keen to get beneath the boxy fur jacket.

I was pretty inexperienced in those days and brought up to be deferential to men, especially older ones, but something told me I had better think of something quick! So I drew a deep breath and turned to the colonel and asked, "By the way, have you ever read *The Confessions of St. Augustine?*"

This had the desired effect. He wrinkled his brow and shook his head and replied, "Actually, no. I don't believe I ever have."

So I began most enthusiastically to expound on the absolutely *fascinating* life of the bishop of Hippo, his mother Monica, and I was just building to the story of the stolen pears, when the colonel suddenly made an apology, realizing the lateness of the hour, and beat a hasty retreat. Phew!

I was saying a silent prayer of thanksgiving as I wriggled into my nightgown, when I heard a voice coming down the crack of the berth above mine. "I say," hoarsely whispered a man from on high, "*jolly* good show!"

It turned out that the colonel was the commander of the young pilot in the berth above me. He was congratulating me at my "wizard" ingenuity in escaping the advances of an experienced old goat. He thought the whole thing was marvelous. I finally fell asleep, rocking in the train, with my red-covered St. Augustine under my pillow. (I still have it.)

The next morning I met the young pilot in the dining car, but I never saw the colonel again. However, soon the train was drawing into Brandon. I hurried back to my seat, which had reappeared, to put my things together.

Across the aisle sat a white-collared Roman Catholic priest. He was also an older man with a cherubic Irish face. He was wearing a jaunty straw hat, a boater. He kept beaming at me, knowingly. Finally, when we stood up to get off, he leaned over and put his hand on my arm, patting it vigorously, and said, "My dear young girl, I want you to be knowin', I was prayin' for you every minute!" So you see, St. Augustine had come to the rescue!

St. Augustine and I shared the same birthday, I told you, and he was the one who prayed to God: "Lord, make me chaste, but not yet!" And he also said that love was the beauty of the soul.

So the written word surely is not to be despised, if it can unite us so intimately through time. How surprised the man might have been to think that some girl, 1500 years later, would be reading his thoughts on a speeding conveyance crossing a continent that hadn't even yet been discovered.

"But," you persisted in asking gently, "which was better, to live something or to read about living something?"

I put my hand into your big warm one. The shock of being alive in the present moment swept over me. It was so strong that I can close my eyes at this instant and be there with all my senses. Something lifted it up into "magical time," which differs from ordinary memory in that I suspect even the passing of time will not change its immediacy. It is "once upon a time," always. I think I know what you were trying to teach me.

We chatted on, always learning something new about each other. I told you about the Christmas I spent in Gstaad when I was ten, when I made that experiment with time. I decided that night to make an appointment with myself on the Christmas night that I would be thirty-two years old. So I tried to concentrate into a psychic time capsule all that I was feeling and experiencing that night as I lay on the wooden bed in the hotel. I still see clearly the position of the bureau, the falling snow dimly reflected by the mirror above it. I remember my gifts, especially an orange-colored fountain pen and a bottle of ink! A new pack of cards, a board game called *Mensch ärger Dich nicht!* (Man, don't get upset!), and two new sweaters. I remember my parents and my grandmother sitting and playing the game with me in the bedroom as a special concession. I promised myself never to forget what it felt like to be a child, when you didn't feel much like one inside. I hoped that I would have a home, a real home, where I belonged.

Through the years I would remember the appointment, and I kept it, though I had to lock myself into the bathroom to do so. And I leaned my head against the wall and wept. It was not a happy place or a happy time. But I unlocked the memories of that childhood moment, and wondered how my own children would look back on their sorrows.

All too often, such immediate moments are painful and traumatic ones. They represent scars and wounds in the psyche which can bring grief, shame, guilt, anger, resentment boiling up out of the personal unconscious and, like hidden currents, force us off course and bring us face to face with people, events, and emotions we had in no way anticipated. So the process itself is a familiar one to most of us, but that moment on the beach, and, by extension, the cumulative experience of Sophia on Iona hint at the unexpected collapsing of time into joy. Not a joy for grabbing, but rather one for visiting. Music, subtle fragrances, art can conjure this way—who knows how it happens, since each of us is different, but the secret has to lie in keeping still, fully aware for a few seconds, in the midst of life, of the Absolute breaking through into the relative, eternity invading the present with the immediacy of just being.

Instead of reading this in a book, put down the book, and be. Feel yourself the center of a circle radiating in all directions into infinity. Collect the moment into a drop of nectar at that center, and then look through the membrane of consciousness which separates your inner and outer worlds. If you are on a bus, pull in the bus and its passengers, and the street, and the houses, and the town, and the country, and so on and on, into that one drop of total awareness of the present moment, unique and significant despite its seeming insignificance. Make the time and the place *conscious*, then invite the Divine Guest to participate in it. Maybe God would like to ride on a bus! Maybe it is time to let the Divine out of the churches and temples and into the world! It was hard enough to share one's religion with others when Jesus was born, and for many it still is, but it is human folly to think that we could or should do otherwise. Again, as Ramakrishna pointed out, we place sticks on top of the water and think we have divided it! I suspect that rediscovering the sacred all about us, with the help of Sophia, is the spiritual task of this new eon. As Jung remarked, God is probably not all that interested in theology.

Anyway, such a moment is a moment of choice, an act of will, an invitation to the Sacred to partake and

incarnate in the commonplace through the playful grace
of Sophia, who will unite the two by giving them meaning. If you are on a bus, you are on a journey from a
"here" to a "there," from a cause to an effect, riding
a hyphen between a hidden and a revealed experience.
If you are in the kitchen, you are an alchemist transforming one form of life into another. If you are in bed,
you are at the edge of two worlds, the conscious and
the unconscious. If you are making love, you are partaking in the outer *coniunctio* that symbolizes the entire creative act of God and creation, for to "make" love
is to create love. In any case, this heightened awareness
is the gift that we give back to the universe. In turn,
Sophia's gift is to render not only our environment trans-
lucent, but to connect events unfolding in our life with
a deeper source. It is as if the circulation throughout
our own individual Tree of Life, as in our bodies, comes
back to the heart of the matter to pulse out afresh with
inner growth and insight. Then things begin to shine
from within, not all the time, but in little magic
glimpses, and we begin to experience what the poet A.
W. Bamberger wrote, "There's a part of the sun in the
apple, a part of the moon in a rose. There's a part of
the flaming Pleiades in everything that grows."

Speaking of alchemy, my father used to tell an amus-
ing true story that illustrates this kind of living alchemy.
Many years ago, he was in San Francisco as a young man
and was visiting Chinatown. There he dined with friends
at a restaurant. The main course was a serving of Pe-
king duck, and it was so exceptionally delicious that my
father, himself an enthusiastic and appreciative person,
asked to meet the chef. Duly, he was taken into the kit-

chen and introduced to a very old Chinese man who spoke little English. My father shook his hand and thanked him for the meal and then asked him for the recipe. The chef shook his head wisely and smiled. "Kind sir," he replied, "the preparation of this duck took three days, with many different stages. In fact, in China we say that when this much attention has been paid to a duck, it has not died at all. It has been translated!"

So, perhaps, that time with you on the White Strand was such a translation, a simple moment shooting out and connecting the very cosmos with the grain of sand quivering on one of my eyelashes.

Reluctantly, we packed our few things, and headed back to the hotel. It had been such a special time for both of us. We knew that we would be leaving Iona the following day. We also knew that we had been there before and would somehow come again. In the meantime, we would carry Iona in the thoughts of our hearts. The "Land of Pure Bliss" is safe within us.

After supper, we again had our coffee in the lounge, sitting in the comfy overstuffed armchairs. Beside me was a bookshelf filled with an assortment of ancient novels of the inimitable variety peculiar to British hotels, mostly published in the 1020s and '30s. I spied a dilapidated anthology of verse and pulled it out, while you were getting yourself a nightcap of brandy. It fell open at one of my favorite poems, written by a man whose work had been lost and then miraculously rediscovered in the late nineteenth century. Never had the words meant as much to me as at this moment:

Iona calling us back

WONDER

How like an Angel came I down!
   How bright are all things here!
When first among his Works I did appear
   O how their Glory did me crown!
The World resembled his ETERNITY,
   In which my Soul did walk;
And ev'ry thing that I did see
   Did with me talk.

The Skies in their Magnificence,
   The lovely lively Air,
O how divine, how soft, how sweet, how fair!
   The Stars did entertain my Sense;
And all the Works of God so bright and pure,
   So rich and great, did seem,
And if they ever must endure
   In my Esteem.

A Nativ Health and Innocence
   Within my Bones did grow,
And while my God did all his Glories show
   I felt a vigor in my Sense
That was all SPIRIT: I within did flow
   With Seas of Life like Wine;
Nothing in the World did know
   But 'twas Divine.

                    Thomas Traherne (1637-1674)

Every time that the powers of the soul
come in contact with created things, they
receive the created images and likenesses
from the created things and absorb them.
In this way arises the soul's knowledge of
created things. Created things can not
come nearer to the soul than this, and the
soul can only approach created things by
the voluntary reception of images. And it
is through the presence of the image that
the soul approaches the created world: for
the image is a thing which the soul
creates with her own powers. Does the
soul want to know the nature of a
stone—a horse—a man? She forms an
image.
      Meister Eckhart, Mystische Schriften

Virtutes divinae in res diffusae.
(Divine powers are diffused in things.)
      Cornelius Agrippa
      von Nettesheim

For oft, when on my couch I lie
    In vacant or in pensive mood
They flash upon that inward eye
    Which is the bliss of solitude
And then my heart with pleasure fills
And dances with the daffodils.
      William Wordsworth

X

Meeting Mercy Muchmore

It was our last day on Iona. Everything a deep slate-blue and streaked by grey slices of cloud and water. The air cold, hollow with a fresh wetness, and whitecaps countering the dark of the tide. Abruptly, I left you at the breakfast table, needing to go out once more and listen to an invisible voice calling. As always, you were understanding. You smiled and let me go.

I put on a wool cap and goatskin gloves, in addition to my parka, and took Woodstock, my Scottish cromag, and set forth pushed from the back by a northerly wind. Here and there cold drops hit my face, and I pulled up my hood. It was cold! But in my heart I felt a warmth and an excitement. I headed for Eithne's Fold, convinced more than ever that I must have once lived on Iona, that, in fact, I was walking over earth that held my bones snugged away somewhere, and by golly, here I was walking over them. The very thought made me joyful, and I prayed God that I would be allowed back in lives hence, or even at the hour of my death to be given one last flight of spirit over these Blessed Isles, the Hebrides. To fly over Skye and Lewis and Harris, to skim through

the dark green hollows of Mull, and roll over Ardnam-
urchan, play with the seals off Coll and Tiree, but come
back, ever and ever, across the silver waters to the Iona
of my heart.

I chose to go to Eithne's Fold because the legend is
that the monks of old would sometimes sit there feeling
an inner warmth and comfort, even smelling a mysterious fragrance of flowers. I had to follow my map to
find it, but soon I was there. It was a green enclosure,
cool and wet.

And somehow I imagined I heard Mercy Muchmore,
my personalized Sophia, the Fairy Godmother of my
childhood, the voice of my own comforter, speaking
firmly within me.

I can only attempt to put some of this into words, because most of my thoughts had the quality of reverie.
I think it began with the realization of what "Muchmore" really means in Gaelic. It means *muc mhor* or
"Great Pig," one of the most ancient depictions of the
old Celtic mother goddess, also known as Ceridwen. It
seemed strange that such a name had surfaced in the
first place. To this day in Europe the pig is a good luck
symbol, especially at New Year's Eve, when to touch
one is specially auspicious. In Germany, Switzerland,
and Austria little marzipan pigs abound in the candy
stores at this time. The English words "much more" were
a serendipity implying that, indeed, there is much more
to life than we normally realize—perhaps good fortune
depends on understanding this. At any rate I enjoyed
the pun.

Next came more thoughts about the nature of the "loving eye." If the time the Self lives in is "once upon a time" and the space the Self lives in is the *temenos*, then surely the eye of the Self is the Third Eye. Then I remembered that after Adam and Eve left Eden with their prize of consciousness, their sons Cain and Abel fell into a deadly argument. The penalty for the slaying of Abel was the mark placed upon the forehead of Cain. Whatever other explanations there may be for it, the fact remains that this mark crossed out the Third Eye. The truth of this profound myth (besides hinting at the subsequent split between nomadic and agricultural people and their religious attitudes, as Joseph Campbell has pointed out) lies in implying that it is the conscious ego who looks through our two eyes and perceives a world of dualities and painful choices. All our senses seem to function in stereo. Even the serpents, ida and pingala, are two. So the secret of union might be seen to be the *shushumna*, the subtle wand or staff of energy rising through the spine—the wand or staff, our potential comforter, which is that in us upon which those serpents twine.

I plucked at the grass and heaved a big sigh. Why was it all so hard, so difficult? Why the wars and killing, the drugs, pollution, and now AIDS? What could any one person do to help change things for the better? It was hard to grasp what seemed to be the answer: "You can only work on yourself. Start there. Your consciousness or that of anybody else's is like the widow's mite—it is all you have to give. Nothing is wasted! But that little bit gets added to all the other little bits, and slowly and inexorably, the light increases and feeds the aura, the noösphere that Teilhard de Chardin described as being about the earth. It is absolutely true that by working on your own shadow, you withdraw it from the collective pool of destructive and unconscious energy. So take heart." Then I heard the words "Remember Louise!" So I thought about Louise, the Louise of my childhood.

Louise was my Grandma King's personal maid. She had come into my grandmother's employ at the age of sixteen around the turn of the century. She was a French peasant girl, daughter of a brickmaker, and she came for her interview in bare feet. My grandparents were touring France at the time when my mother was a little girl. Grandma King was to become an anomaly of sorts: a well-to-do widow who lived a gracious life doing absolutely nothing in the most charming of ways. Louise remained her maid for over sixty years, always keeping her place, sewing, packing, doing up her mistress's hair in little leather twists at night and combing out the white waves the next morning. Louise was short, squat, and taciturn, and my grandmother was the picture of Victorian elegance to her dying day. They were an odd pair, each totally dependent upon the other.

Louise brought up my mother and then tried her hand on me whenever I was available. From time to time, the two women would sail to Europe, and Grandma would set herself up in various fine hotels and make herself available. I think it was her attempt, perhaps, to give me some sense of family and continuity. I remember she always traveled with a beautiful silver teapot, handmade of old Boston hammered silver. When teased by my father, who felt there must be teapots available anywhere, she would rebuke him, saying, "I think it's important that Alice should know where she comes from." So for quite a while, I believed I came into this world poured out of that teapot!

Louise would sometimes tell me stories of her childhood as she ironed out Grandma's pink satin lingerie in her own more modest hotel bedroom, and I assumed that it was the story about the stars that Mercy Muchmore was alluding to, because this is the one that came up in my mind. Louise had told me that in her village they believed that the sky was a vast inverted bowl, and that what we called stars were really chinks or holes in the bowl through which you could see the streaming light of the gold in heaven. The image was a very powerful one for me, too. I never forgot it.

It seems to suggest that we might be mistaken in always thinking that we have to struggle and achieve our growth, and that the secret of inner growth might be better seen as an *allowing* rather than a frantic fighting for perfection—a cracking or perforating of our shell, allowing the light to begin streaming out through us. I pictured being sort of a sieve for God.

This would mean a surrendering of arrogance and a submission of the conscious ego to the Divine Guest within us. After all, Christ did not choose perfected people to be his disciples; quite the contrary. And he was the one to remind us to "consider the lilies—neither do they toil nor spin, yet surely Solomon in all his glory is not clad like one of these." In other words, trust the process; don't put so many unnecessary obstacles in the way. Look, even at yourself, with a humorous tolerance and a loving eye. A loving eye then would extend to people and situations, to seeing beauty in the very fragility and even the ugliness in the world, to let oneself be touched even by the artificial lace on a woman's cotton slip—a small token of Venus, nevertheless.

To live in the world and give all the fruits of your action to God is the path of karma yoga. This means *all*. Failures included. In the West, we tend to quickly scrutinize and judge, only offering up the wee bit of good we deem to have achieved. Then we keep all the bad stuff and it piles up and up. No wonder we get depressed and end up in the therapist's office. I remembered then the funny dream I had about Father Tom Berry, the ecologist. I had just visited his splendid library containing all the sacred texts of all the world's religions:

> Tom Berry turns to me and says, "By the way, did I show you my Godmachine?" No, he hadn't. "Oh," he says, "I meant to. It's such a convenience."
>
> He leads me to a black metal box with a shelf in it, and a device in the middle. "I can take any of these books and just place it in here, so. When I flip on the switch, the book will turn to crystal and the words that are true in the sight of God will instantly turn to gold." He demonstrates this. One book has only one sentence, another several slices of gold. I am fascinated. Then Tom Berry says, "You know, you could put a day of your life in there, or a week, or a year." The idea makes me very uneasy. Seeing this, he adds, "But only on one condition. You have to realize the value of the dark parts of the crystal. It is they that hold the gold."

Somehow that made me feel better when I woke up and thought about it.

Inversely, the voice seemed to go on, if we are by true nature beings of light, then wherever we make a mistake out of wilfulness [sin] or ignorance, we block that light. This is the meaning, surely, to the myths of Achilles' Heel and the leaf that fell on Siegfried's back, when he tried to make himself invincible by bathing in dragon's blood. These are our blind spots. So wherever the winds of fate blow, they are apt to get caught or hooked in our vulnerable places. Here is where the individual "work" lies.

I gave another big sigh, and the voice ceased to speak, so I got up and looked about. Suddenly I realized that I had been sitting in the very spot I had sat in at least ten years previously. Sat and prayed, and yes, cried as well, out of my utter loneliness. I remembered another poem written at that time.

BEGGAR

Some beg for money
some beg for bread
that they may live—
but strangest,
surely
is that poor beggar
who must beg
to give!

And I thought of you and how much I had to be grateful for!

"And didn't I always tell you to trust, to believe?" chided Mercy Muchmore. "The spring and the ocean meet in the arches of rainfall and undercurrents of intent. Your tears, your sighs of despair and torrents of

passion and emotion keep you and everyone alive and
yearning. Drop by drop by drop the tears of the lonely
fall on the heart of Wisdom, and to each soul Sophia
reaches out her comforting hands:

> *I walk through the wood*
> *through the mist*
> *and I am calling, calling*
> *your name—*
> *but no one answers.*
>
> *And I have flowers in my arms!*

"Here," and her voice spoke more gruffly, "pick up
that stone. Let it be a covenant between us." She could
have told me to pick up that spoon, or that box, or that
ashtray, or that glove—it makes no difference. The simple things around you at home, all are laden with wisdom at many different levels. You have a spoon, a
wooden kitchen spoon. Every time you pick it up, you
could remember where you got it and when, and to fully
explain that you would have to give the entire history
of your life, and that of all your ancestors, because it
was all the world that brought you to that shop, at that
particular time, in that particular place. So every commonplace "thing" connects you to the universe. Every
thing is a "souvenir," a reminder of import.

"The spoon isn't even here. It's at home by your stove,
but you know which one I am talking about, don't you?
So you brought it with you." She showed me that it is
in me because I paid attention to it. It connects me to
whoever made the spoon, to the tree it came from,
however many years of sun-in-the-wood ago, and on and
on. The spoon can teach us about its process of receiv-

ing and giving, and it is not unlike our precious ego that can dip into and distribute the gifts of our Godself, or bring back to it the gifts of our experience made conscious.

"This simple wisdom of spoons is hiding out on all the tables in all the homes and restaurants of the world," continued Mercy Muchmore, "even in the hands of philosophers and theologians busy with words and words and more words explaining the meaning of life! Their wisdom is linear, mine is imaginal." (No, not to be confused with imaginary!) *Both* are necessary, but this way has been sorely neglected. It is not a way of constructing, but rather an unveiling by the inward eye. Such thoughts have come down almost to a whisper in the dreams of men and women, and are often set aside because such dreams seem unrealistic and impractical. But as William Blake wrote: "What is now proven was once only imagined." What psychology today calls "magical thinking" is an insult! Sophia is always practical. *Prakriti* is another of her names (the Hindu womb goddess of matter).

"I'll tell you a secret and promise that you'll tell! *Everywhere is here. Everywhen is now.*" I had to laugh, despite myself. In my mind's eye, I could just see her emphatic nod of the head.

I stretched slowly and decided Iona was making me a mite balmy. So I stood up and decided to push on once more for the Hermit's Cell, the ring of stones at the west of the island, just to say good-bye. The grass shone an eerie electric green, and the heather stood out pink and purple and violet against that deep slate-blue of the dark

Searching for the Hermit's Cell

air. In fact, the clouds were so low they were turning to mist as they touched the higher rocks. I began to take note of the direction the heather was nodding to orient myself to the abbey, no longer in sight.

Somehow I found my way back to the stone circle and perched there on a rock. It seems Mercy Muchmore had a bit more to say. "If you can practice listening to the wisdom of the commonplace, honoring it for its simplicity, little by little, you will begin to see through the veil of the *unus mundus*. And for those who begin to experience this, the fear of death will lessen, for you are living in a time when more and more people will be dying consciously. You all know theoretically that you will die someday, but to die slowly of a terminal disease is an accelerator and aids the speeding up of a sense of priorities. The more people collectively hover between worlds, the thinner the veil will become even for others, and the easier it will be for me to show myself. My stone will come alive, and the concealed dove of wisdom will fly out of it, and the wings at the top of my wand will move, and the Tree of Light that is in you all can come to life. For I am the plant that grows in both your worlds that Jung spoke of in your dream. I am truly she.

"Invite the Sacred to participate in your joy in little things, as well as in your agony over the great ones. There are as many miracles to be seen through a microscope as through a telescope. Start with little things seen through the magnifying glass of wonder, and just as a magnifying glass can focus the sunlight into a burning beam that can set a leaf aflame, so can your focused wonder set you ablaze with insight. Find the light in each other and just fan it.

"Try it! Practice! Find one thing to praise in every day and by saying grace (*gratia*) or thank you, you will receive grace. It's that simple. Just do little things with great love, as Mother Teresa says. Then see what happens."

It seemed like a lot to remember. I got up. It was time to try to find my way back through the cold wet mist. I marveled at the mixture of wisdom and nonsequiturs that seemed to be my Fairy Godmother's approach. It seemed so scattered. Then I remembered the words "I am scattered throughout the world, and in gathering me together, thou gatherest together thyself." They could just as well apply to Sophia. In fact, the "Anamnesis of Sophia" (re-membering) seems to involve finding lost pieces to a picture puzzle in different parts of the house of the psyche—under the sofa, at the back of a table drawer, and on and on and on, as she would say! I hope I will be forgiven. They really do talk in circles.

With the help of Woodstock, I was now climbing up and down, trying hard to avoid the squelchy, boggy parts underfoot, and yet not miss the occasional goldening of the mist as the clouds scudded and thinned below the sun. I stopped and breathed in the gold.

Then abruptly I came down to good old reality and found myself in a very real and dense fog. Highly symbolic, I thought to myself. A sameness of green and heather and rock stretched in all directions. It was now almost lunch time, and we had a ferry to make off Mull. I could imagine you trying not to worry, probably taking our suitcases out to the hall for the hotel car to take

St. Oran's Chapel

down to the jetty. I stood still and breathed in just a little more gold. Then I remembered to look at the bending of the grass and the nodding bog cotton. It had been a northerly wind when I left, and I only hoped it still was. So I headed east, hoping that my sensation function would function sensationally! Eventually I came to the wire fence, slipped through the familiar opening, and by keeping it in sight trusted it to lead me to the grass-covered causeway that had once enclosed a water supply for the monks. It would lead to the youth camp and the road above the abbey. Before long, I met some very shy sheep, and then some foggy cows, crossed the small burn, and the words "Coffee Shop" appeared, and then the abbey loomed out of the mist. I crossed the road and stopped in at St. Oran's Chapel, the oldest intact building on Iona and surrounded by the graves of the sixty kings.

The chapel is small, simple and whitewashed inside. I sat down on a wooden bench and noticed that I was flanked by two graves on either side. I surely remembered to say thanks, which wasn't hard, so full was my heart for my life. I looked at the brass cross on the wall holding its sacred secrets and saw a tiny bunch of flowers in a wee grail that someone had placed there. A sign of Sophia's unseen presence. I prayed that I could do justice to what I had learned on Iona, and that together with you I could return home and learn more, much more about Sophia. And then I laughed. Mercy Muchmore had done it again!

*Delight is a secret....delight has a glancing,
dancing, penetrative quality, the quality of
Sophia the consort of God, as when she sings—
    "From the beginning I was with Him,
    forming all things: And was delighted
    everyday, playing before Him at all
    times: Playing in the world; and my delights
    were to be with the children of men."*

*Playing in the world! That is what Wisdom does.
And this is what they miss, those sad, resigned
ones....the will-driven, over-masculinized betrayers of
life.*

*Delight is a mystery. And the mystery is this:
to plunge boldly into the brilliance and immediacy of
living, at the same time as utterly surrendering to
that which lies beyond space and time; to see life
translucently...*

*Alan McGlashan
The Savage and Beautiful Country*

*Silly, adj. Simple, harmless, foolish. (E.) The
word has much changed its meaning. It
meant 'timely,' then lucky, happy, blessed...Allied to O. Lat.* sollus, *favorable,
complete; also to Lat.* salvus, *whole, safe.*
    *Walter W. Skeat, An Etymological
    Dictionary of the English Language*

XI

Oringing home the Oove

We left Iona, or did we? The crossing was rough with spray swishing over the sides and swirling over the rusty green paint of the iron deck. It made our lips taste of salt. Heavy chains of water kept falling behind us, and we had to hold on to keep from falling overboard. Most of the crofter women, dressed respectably in coats and hats, sought the diminutive smoke-filled lounge, but the Community people were dressed as we were, in rugged parkas and carrying huge backpacks, and all wuffled up in woolen scarves and hats of every color and description. The Wild Man, as I admiringly dubbed him, collected our tickets. He was a big man and had the handsome look of some Celtic Cuchulainn about him, with his wet locks and great unwashed paws and a jersey frayed with wear that hadn't seen a washtub since it was knitted. He strode the deck in his enormous gumboots, smiling into the teeth of the gale. It was nice to know such a man still existed.

We picked up our rental car at Fionnphort and drove across Mull—one of the most desolate roads I know— and looked through the furious wagging of the wind-

153

shield wiper at the dark, green-grey and stormy mountains brooding and looming around us. We both settled
into our thoughts, occasionally squeezing each other's
hand in gratitude for having shared the adventure. We
were now on our way to "over the sea to Skye."

As we drove, I thought of how many goddesses there
are in all the mythologies of the world, and how, like
the gods, they seemed to carry projections of various
psychic functions. Slowly I began to realize that the goddesses, in many instances, matched the various levels of
the chakras, so that the earthy and chthonic ones resonated to the lower chakras, and the merciful and loving ones, to the heart, and so forth. And yet they were
all variations of the feminine, culminating, it would
seem, in those goddesses specifically associated with
wisdom.

Scathach (pronounced Ski-a), the goddess of Skye, ran
a school for heroes, no less, and Cuchulainn was one
of her students. He learned so well that, in the end, he
overcame her and sired a daughter (perhaps a Hebridean version of the patriarchy overcoming the matriar-
chy). In any case, Scathach would have resonated with
the power chakra. Kali, the great Mother Goddess, the
many-armed black goddess of India, would perhaps
unite the highest and the lowest chakras in the circulation of energy. These goddesses, like the gods, remain
archetypal personifications of universal processes—not
meant to be taken literally at a higher level of understanding—and though the names change from culture
to culture, the processes associated with them do not.
We are only just beginning to appreciate the fact that
one cannot kill an archetype, and that these "gods" and

"goddesses" *in that understanding* are alive and well and living in our own psyches, though we may give them other names. Just comprehending this much might have saved the world from the dreadful iconoclasms of history, in which so much beautiful art was destroyed through sheer ignorance!

Sophia, or Holy Wisdom, is not usually thought of as a goddess, since that would sound far too pagan for Christians, even early ones. Yet she was considered co-creator with God in the Old Testament, and other cultures found it easier to regard her as one. No matter what name we call her, for us she is divine since she is universal, and we personify her with the title *Hagia Sophia* or "Holy Wisdom" and find her hidden in the symbols of the stone, representing manifest earth, and the serpents of the spinal energy, and the dove pointing to the wings of higher consciousness, a consciousness uniting opposites. Sophia, as Holy Spirit, Holy Breath, or kundalini, becomes the Mother of God, the *theotokos*, because it is the Sophia in any of us that brings about our inner rebirth. This is the result of her uniting the *ha* and *tha* (in Sanskrit, Sun and Moon), as in "Hatha" Yoga, or bringing about the *hierosgamos*, the sacred marriage of the king and queen, gold and silver, etc., referred to by the alchemists. In the body, according to yoga, she brings about the union of the secretions of the pineal and pituitary glands, the *ida* and *pingala*, and on and on, through all the opposites needing reunion. All of this is the divine task of Sophia, of the Kundalini in the marriage of Shakti and Shiva for the Hindus, or the task of Shekinah for the Kabbalists. That inner marriage was, and is, a holy secret of the "magic wand" of the caduceus, and it is ideally mirrored outwardly by sex, love, and marriage between man and woman. For me it brought to life the biblical verses that read: "And he went in unto her and knew her." So the *coniunctiones* that abound in all of manifest life point to the same process within the psyche, within the soul.

The key to this process on the physical level was discovered of old to be breathing. "Cleanse me by the inspiration of thy Holy Spirit," we pray, perhaps not realizing that hidden in the word is the root of *spirare*, "to breathe," and perhaps not remembering that our left and right nostrils conduct the air, the *pneuma*, to the opposite hemispheres of our brain. So, while for the anatomist it is oxygen that keeps our systems alive, for the esotericist it is *prana*, the invisible spirit in life that nourishes the reborn Self in the womb of our souls. And it is this energy that is symbolized by the glyph of Aquarius, the waves of the Holy Spirit being poured out of the Holy Grail as a gift to the new aeon, the Aquarian Age.

I was certain, as we drove closer and closer on the wet, shining, serpentine road to Craignure that rainy day, that this might be an area where science and theology could also come together, but it would take a translating and experiencing of many symbols, and an understanding of the ongoing meaning that they point to. As the Sufis say, a symbol is a theophany of the Absolute in the relative. Such truths can only be hidden really in "types and images," because this is a code which lasts; while languages change in meaning, images and geometry do not. Actually, all we need to know is locked up securely within our own bodies, but we need a key that can translate the algebra of the archetypal or universal processes (verbs!) that exist within our own body and the extended one of the goddess, our wise Mother Earth.

That key is to be found in the symbolic language of astrology and within the mystery of our own psyches, as I have tried to point out in my work, *Jungian Symbolism in Astrology*. In the Western world, finding it and using it was the great opus or the Great Work of the alchemist, and to a large extent today it is the focus of certain psychologies and of all the esoteric understandings of religions. To medieval thinking, that such a quest could be undertaken outside of the Mother Church was dangerous and heretical because it gave too much power to individuals and not enough power and social control to the Church. Even today it is a dangerous pursuit if it is undertaken without love and humility on the part of the ego. But Sophia is a loving and cheerful and kind presence. She blossoms only at a level beyond the heart chakra and thus is unattainable for power plays, yet she can neither bloom nor give fruit if she is not rooted in the depths of earth. This is her consummate gift, the revelation to us of a "spirituous earth."

I heaved a great sigh. The opus seems so out of reach! And then I heard good old Mercy Muchmore laughing and saying, "Keep with the little things, one day at a time. Sufficient unto the day is the wisdom thereof."

We followed a bend in the road and came to a very sudden halt. In seconds we found ourselves literally in a sea of sheep, their black and white heads bobbing around us. We rolled down our windows and listened to the baa-ing, the wooly shuffling, and the high clattering of their little hooves on the road. The shepherd grinned and waved his cromag, and his two border collies went to work. In a matter of minutes, the dogs had them off the road, making the way clear. We watched a stray being rounded up. The dog would bound ahead, then turn and lie down facing the sheep, which would then think twice about going in that direction! Little by little the stray was forced back to where she belonged. With a congratulatory wave we drove on, and shortly took our place in the line of cars waiting for the ferry—and for fish and chips to come.

The next ten days teemed with the beauty of the isles and the Highlands. Nowhere are there more beautiful colors. Now we were where the bracken grows. The fern was turning orange, the rowan trees hung with red berries, and the last of the foxgloves lined the roadways.

In no time, though, we were back home, just in time to catch the full glory of a New England autumn. And before long, I remembered my promise to seek out Sophia's other names. Actually, I have been gathering them for over forty years, but I had not appreciated that that indeed was what I had been doing. So out came my commonplace books, and soon the library was strewn with open volumes. I had to laugh when, in one of Jung's works, I came across this quotation from one of the alchemists, "One book opens another." And as I worked, the synchronicities (always a sign of Sophia) began to manifest. Here are some of them:

—I returned to answering a volume of letters from readers of my first book. To catch up, I had the kind assistance of a young woman and neighbor, Nicky

Hearon. Two letters, in particular, dealt with the symbolism of the dove. When dictation was over, I offered to take Nicky home. While we were driving along, she said how helpful it would be for women to know that there was a feminine archetype, to which they could relate, that was loving rather than resentful, that could give women a sense of dignity by restoring the feminine to its rightful place in the Godhead. And as she was speaking, we turned a bend in the road and right in front of the car, *walking* with a firm and unalarmed tread, was a pure white dove with pink legs. It strode ahead, up a small incline, turned and walked right back at us. I rolled down the window and she walked past the car while Nicky and I gripped each other, grateful that there were two of us, because nobody would have believed the tale had we been alone! Since then the doves (there are two) have been sighted three times, once on the roof of our house. We must presume that somebody is breeding them in the area, but that the dove appeared at that particular moment was a perfect example of the coincidence of an outer event with inner meaning, which is Jung's definition of the word "synchronicity."

—Around that time a dove-like form appeared in the frost on our windowpane. It was about eighteen inches long. We photographed it.

—I received a phone call, and a subsequent letter from a delightful Hungarian woman, Helen Pellathy, who attended some classes I gave on Jung years ago. She had had a dream.

It was a flat meadow, covered with stones, rocks, rounds and squares, in different sizes and many colors. You had a twig in your hand and planted it among the stones—it

started to grow—became a tree—a large trunk—and in
the middle a green bough started to grow and grow
towards the sky, lovely green color, covering the sky. Full
of wonder I asked you—how did you do it? "Simple, I
watered it with warm water," you said.

—The next day a Unicef catalog arrived. On the front
was the stylized picture of a flower whose petals are
turning to little doves.

—A tiny dove appears in a crystal we have in our meditation room. Also discovered by Nicky.

—I reach for a book called *The Flaming Door* by
Eleanor C. Merry, a book I have not yet read, and find
the following quotation. I am so excited about it I call
the home of Chris Bamford. His friend, Tadea Dufault,
who traveled with him and us to Iona last summer, says
they have the book. She goes to fetch it. A bookmark
is placed in that very page. Here is what is written:

> . . . let me tell of one other legend whose origin is un-
> known to me. . . it is a relic of some heart's deep brood-
> ing, born of the sea-foam and far horizons of the Western
> Isles—intangible and beautiful, it is the vision of a vision:

> "A certain solitary, whose dwelling-place was on a hill-
> side of the mainland, not very far from Iona, sat one day
> in meditation gazing over the calm sea. Presently he saw,
> rising up majestically in the airy clouds, the glorified
> golden-hued form of St. Columba. The Saint, too, was
> in meditation and created in his thoughts a picture
> which, by reason of the holy power in him that sent it
> forth, became endowed with immortality and purpose.
> It was a picture of the Virgin with the Christ-child in
> her arms. It floated away from the islands, came towards
> the mainland, and spread in lovely colours far and wide
> over the world. Yet it was more than a picture for it

seemed to utter its meaning: *'I am Mary-Sophia, sent forth in this image over all the Earth to bring healing to men who will lose the power to see me as I really am. I will live in their Art till their thoughts raise me again to the Kingdom of the Heavens which are within them on Earth.'* " [Italics mine]

A month later yet another book falls into my hands, a book written in 1910 called *Iona* by Fiona Macleod (William Sharp). In it I find the following words:

> From one man only, on Iona itself, I have heard any allusion to the prophecy as to the Saviour yet to come. . . . with a descending of the Divine Womanhood upon the human heart as a universal spirit descending upon waiting souls. . . .
>
> One of those to whom I allude was a young Hebridean priest, who died in Venice. . . he told me once how as our forefathers and elders believed and still believe, that Holy Spirit shall come again which was once mortally born among us as the Son of God, but then shall be the Daughter of God. "The Divine Spirit shall come again as a Woman. Then for the first time the world will know peace." And when I asked him if it were not prophesied that the Woman is to be born on Iona, he said that if this prophecy had been made it was doubtless of an Iona that was symbolic, but that this was a matter of no moment, for She would rise suddenly in many hearts, and have her habitation among dreams and hopes.

As I perused the reprint of this book, I noticed it was made by "Floris" Books, a Scottish firm, whose logo is a dove! Named for Joachim, no doubt.

These synchronicities are the little winks that fairy godmothers are apt to give along the way for any of us. They are what can make any old day a magical one. They seem to say, at least to me, that we must learn

Off the ferry and on with life

to smile and acknowledge the fact that the *unus mundus* is around all the time, but we have to look *through* this one to perceive it. "There is another world, but it is hidden in this one!" Then, somehow, one gets the impression that Sophia is indeed involved with delight.

This disposition is cosmic, it is alive in the Cosmos and is what I call here the Functional Principle. Some have called these Principles divine qualities, or even names of God; the ancient Egyptians called them Neters, a word cabalistically linked to "nitr" and to "Nature."

Thus the "function" of growth is the concretization of the abstract, just as the creative function is dualization of Unity, and all of Nature is the effect of division.

Analogies and Signatures are the Sage's guides and make him a Magus. This word frightens you, but true Science can only be Magic.

R.A. Schwaller de Lubicz

God, from the beginning of the world has created things holy and pure, and they need not be consecrated by man. It is for us by becoming holy, to recognize the holiness of God in external nature.

Philosophia Occulta

Everything that is within can be known by what is without.

Paracelsus

A little bird told me.
Folk saying

XII

A Rose by Any Other Name

You were in the kitchen nook savoring a cup of tea. We had just brought in the geraniums as a precaution against an early frost, and now they were hanging in the windows providing a green, stained-glass effect between the yellow checked curtains. The sun was glancing off your white hair. A plate of buttermilk scones that I had baked from the little recipe book you bought me on Skye lay before you on a blue and white plate upon the round table. I drew in a breath of gratitude, and remembered the Fairy Godmother's adage: the secret of happiness is to know when you're happy. Well, I knew I was happy. Snuffy MacDuff, our cairn puppy, bounded in with what you call "a burst of hoppiness," his own version of joy. I told you that I had attempted a few words on the subject of Sophia's other names. We ended up with a lively discussion of labels and language and how easily we can be drawn into confusion. It might help to explain that just as there is only one yin and one yang, there is only one feminine and one masculine principle, but both have many, many manifestations, and human gender is only one of these. So I handed you an attempt that I had written showing that the function

of Sophia appears in many other cultures. What follows
are only a very *few* examples:

> *anima mundi* (soul of the earth)
> *lumen naturae* (light of nature)
> Queen or Wind of the South, Queen of Sheba
>   (alchemy)
> *tella mater* (mother earth)
> The Woman clothed with the Sun (New Testament)
> Spenta, Daena (Zoroastrian)
> *ruh muhammadan*, Fatima (Shi'ite)
> Maat (Egyptian)
> Metis (Greek)
> Azbaanadleehi (Woman of Changing that I) Navaho
> Tara (Tibetan Buddhist)
> Dame Kinde (Old English)
> Kwan Yin (Chinese)
> Shakti, Prakriti (Hindu)
> Shekinah, Chokmah (Judaic)
> Brid (Celtic)
> Mother Goose

To recapitulate: all of them, in one way or another,
remind us that it takes the feminine aspect of wisdom
to find the sacred in the commonplace.

No matter what our religion or lack thereof, if we live
in the Western world we are psychically affected by the
mythology surrounding us, because it affects us social-
ly and culturally, as well. (A simple example would be
the Christmas shopping season.) The mythology of the
Holy Trinity which was shaped in the fifth century A.D.
has affected us subtly but profoundly. That removing
of the feminine from the Godhead was as illogical as

declaring the world to be all yang without yin and, as
Jung has shown, whenever an excessive attitude is consciously identified with, the opposite is constellated in
the unconscious. If only we could understand and remember this; if only the fundamentalists of all the religions in the world could grasp this, we might make a
smoother transition into the era to come. Jung pointed
out that through an excessive identification of masculine,
extroverted ego intellect with virtuous righteousness,
goodness, and light, the feminine and darkness (i.e. "the
devil") became constellated in the Western unconscious.
By the time the Middle Ages came and went, women,
matter, and the devil conflated in the minds of many
as sources of evil and temptation. An elaborate hell was
located below ground in the earth, complete with
flames, demons, and monsters—a concretization, if ever
there was one. Poor Mother Earth! The negative projections came out in full force with the Inquisition onto
heretics and witches, despite the preceding interim of
the increased worship of the Virgin Mary, which was
due to the influence of chivalry and the troubadours;
this had spread through Europe as the result of contact
with the East through the Crusades. And, despite the
compelling exceptions of such souls as St. Francis and
the subsequent doomed efforts of the Cathars and the
Beguines, Sophia had to go into hiding, and the alchemists who befriended her were forced to work in darkest
secret. It was Paracelsus who wrote, "Moreover the light
of nature is a light that is lit from the Holy Ghost and
goeth not out, for it is well lit, and the light is of a kind
that desireth to burn."

The coming of Protestantism in the sixteenth century
excluded the feminine even further; the worship of Mary

was stopped among Protestants, and the artistic embellishments of Catholicism were swept away in a fury of iconoclasm, and, in many places, destroyed for all time. Religious wars broke out; monasteries and churches were closed and defiled. Thousands of lives were lost. Severity, austerity, and the suppression of carnal pleasures ensued. Even Christmas was abolished! One of my own Puritan ancestors, so the story goes, sat at the Sabbath dinner table, and when his little son praised his mother's good soup, reached over and poured cold water into it.

Nor is this Calvinist attitude gone even in Scotland. I can remember an incident on the Isle of Lewis a few years ago. I was driving a minivan with six young boys and my youngest daughter, all under fifteen inside. We were on a one-track road, with only passing places. To the left and right, nothing but a wasteland of rock and peat bog stretched out in all directions, with not a house or a shepherd's bothy in sight. It was a Sunday. To amuse themselves the kids had been playing seven pennywhistles all at the same time, until I could barely concentrate.

I suggested one of them read the story of Bonnie Prince Charlie, who with his savior Flora MacDonald, are the folk heroes of Scotland. The children quieted down and I drove on slowly, listening myself. Suddenly out of nowhere a dilapidated truck whirled through a passing place and rushed ahead of me and came to a full stop. Out came an irate, bewhiskered man. He berated me, saying he had followed me for "siven males," and did I not know what passing places were for! I apologized for not having looked in the mirror, and then I asked him why he had not sounded his horn. "Whssht, lass, dinna ye ken 'tis the Sabbath? Blow me horn, indeed, and distairb the folk!" However, when I explained that I had been so absorbed in listening to the story of Bonnie Prince Charlie, he softened and gave an understanding smile. *That* explained it. He gave the kids a wave, went back to his truck, and drove off.

To continue, rationalism and the rapid rise of industry in the following two centuries struck another blow against Sophia, despite the efforts of the Romantic movement, and then industrial materialism settled in to pour concrete almost upon our very souls.

But in the last thirty years, a change has been taking place, a slow surge of protest led by a new generation of men and women. If you are reading these words, you are probably one of them. It is a healthy sign. Women are crying out, less in anger now than at the beginning, but still in a quest for a recognition of their contribution towards healing the world. The perilous state of the earth's ecology is awakening us all to the absolute necessity to change our ways. As Jung put it, "The entire world hangs on the thin thread of man's psyche." The enemy is not nature, but mankind.

Again, as Jung has pointed out, during these centuries the East remained the balancing hemisphere. There the feminine, introverted approach to life has never wavered. Yet, for them the trap is the attitude of laissez-faire. Ambition for material progress is largely still unconscious at the collective level, and health, education, and technology have been slow in emerging.

These remarks are grossly oversimplified, to be sure, but in each case, whether East or West, the sticking point has been the relationship to "matter." At the mythological level, the East prays to be delivered from its unreality (Maya) and the West has looked down upon it as something to be manipulated or "zapped." The words, "Thy Kingdom come on earth as it is in heaven" have been misheard. We interpret them as meaning something we have to *do* to matter, rather than looking *through* matter to the divine energy and wisdom concealed within it, the *lumen naturae,* the "light of nature," or the *anima mundi,* "the soul of the world." We have forgotten that our task is less to dominate than to cooperate with nature and to see ourselves as extensions of one another.

These two views constitute opposites crying out for a reconciling third. That third has always existed and has been preserved by the esoteric traditions of all the major religions, by the mystics, and in a way by the obdurate Celtic Christians of the West of Ireland and the West of Britain: Scotland, Wales, and the Hebrides. There in the Gaelic tongue the prayers and songs rose and fell, with a Christian overlay, to an unflagging devotion to Sophia, first called Brith (or Brid), then St. Brigid, the Mary of the Gael. Brid was the goddess of wisdom, flocks, poetry, and laughter!

If all is energy, we have a choice of seeing it as impersonal happenstance, or seeing it through our own evolving consciousness as divine consciousness, as an overwhelming love. "The fires of hell are the flames of God's love rejected," as Dorothy L. Sayers remarked. But using logic, if *all* is consciousness, and consciousness is something we have in common with the divine, *then* all of nature, in its own and varying ways, also has consciousness. This is not plain animism, because the primitive's animism at that level is still fused, as an infant's perception of himself is fused with the environment, a *participation mystique*. What Sophia offers is a view of the earth beyond the ego's arrogance, an empirical experience, at long last, of the Holy all about us. It is akin to what a dedicated gardener may sense. It sheds light on Mary Magdalen, who, of all the women around Jesus, was first to see the risen Christ, thinking he was "the gardener" in the garden.

Another example of Sophia's association with flowers comes to us through one of Wisdom's other personifications, that of Daena in Zoroastrianism. There her particular flower was the rose of a hundred petals. Here we already find the rich symbolism of the rose that traveled West, and which found its way into Christianity through its association with Mary, the mystic rose. We can think also of "The Romance of the Rose," and the Gothic rose windows, and the symbolism of white and red roses. Henri Corbin, writing in his profound book *Spiritual Body and Celestial Earth* has more to say:

> The ancient Persians, too, had a language of flowers, which was a sacred language. Moreover, this delicate and subtle symbolism offers unlimited possibilities to liturgical imagination as well as for rituals of meditation. In their turn, the art of gardens and the cultivation of a garden thus acquire the meaning of a liturgy and a mental actualization of a vision. In this art, flowers play the part of the *materia prima* for alchemical meditation. This means mentally reconstituting Paradise, keeping company with heavenly beings; contemplation of the flowers which are their emblems evoke psychic reactions, which transmute the forms contemplated into energies

corresponding to them; these psychic energies are finally dissolved into states of consciousness, into states of mental vision through which the heavenly Figures appear.

We use flowers as gifts of love, at births, weddings, and funerals, but to contemplate them as guides between the outer world of nature and its hidden meaning could be another good place to start the search for Sophia; a place where the loving eye could find pleasure in the exercise.

Every flower carries a numerical and geometric signature which links it to a planetary or archetypal process. The rose, thus, is a mandala, symbolic of totality. It grows according to the laws discovered by Fibonacci governing an e-curve of growth; its spiraling growth determines that no one leaf will shade another from its share of sunshine. Its signature is the pentagram, the very same we find in the apple or in the proportions of the Golden Mean, the Parthenon, and the chambered nautilus, to mention but a few, and even within the RNA/DNA of our own genetic structure. Making these connections is Sophia's task. *Omnia coniungo.*

Other flowers have three or four petals, or their multiples. The hexagram yields the Star of David, the Shri Yantra, and the harmonious union of masculine and feminine, logos and eros, and on and on, as Mercy Muchmore would say. Truly, Sophia is incandescent, her light illuminates our insight. All that she asks is that we answer the invitation to play her game of hide-and-seek. It is time now that we learn the rules, the how-to, of that game.

In ancient Egypt one of Sophia's prior personifications, hinted at by the presence of her outstretched wings
and a feather on her head, is that of Maat. Maat was
the goddess of cosmic order, the Tao, the dharma, the
wisdom by which the cosmos functions harmoniously
and on time. In ancient Greece, the goddess of wisdom
was Metis, possibly cognate, and the etymology here suggests holy measure and proportion displayed in beauty. In India, her names are Prajna-paramita or Prakriti
and, within us, the great love of the feminine Shakti rising through the kundalini to the embrace of Shiva. Or
we find Krishna, also virgin-born, loving each of the
Gopi maidens, who were called out to bathe with him
in the moonlight. And each returned convinced he had
loved only her, as he loved his consort Rada. Krishna-
consciousness is achieved by the same process as Christ-
consciousness, East and West, there is "only one
way"....

The presence of the feminine is essential to the masculine for spiritual rebirth, and vice versa. Even the
alchemist required a *soror mystica,* a mystical sister, to
perform the opus. To what extent this needs to be "acted
out" is not the issue here, for very often a relationship
between a man and a woman that is tantric or not con-
summated sexually, keeps the process within the vessel
and internalized. Such relationships are most difficult
and yet most rewarding. They are love deeply bound
into friendship, or friendship enfolded in human love.
St. Francis and St. Clare, St. Teresa and St. John of the
Cross come to mind. And the myths of faithful knights
who sleep with their king's wives with a sword lying between them. Such love was idealized in times of chivalry,

when the knight served his fair lady as he would the Virgin on earth. For today, however, the ideal even more difficult to attain is that of a conjugal love growing mutually up through all the chakras!

Sex is indeed the sacred fire, not to be renounced, but to further consciousness level by level through love.

In Tibetan Buddhism, Sophia's name is "Tara," and one of the most exquisite descriptions of her is in a Sadhana paraphrased by a Western Buddhist practitioner, Lex Hixon. Another version of this can be found in Edward Conze's *Buddhist Texts*. Here the source goes by the intriguing name of: *Aryatarabhattarikanamashtottarasatakastotra!*

A SADHANA OF THE GODDESS TARA

Surrounded by the rain forest of the realm where animals live in peace, and where healing herbs grow in abundance, on a meditation seat of sacred kusha grass, radiantly smiling, completely relaxed yet poised with her right foot touching the earth, ready to rise and engage in compassionate action, eternally sixteen, wearing rainbow silks and golden ornaments, Her luminous body, green and delicate as a tender shoot, the Divine Wisdom Mother Tara sits in a circle of sunlight beside a lotus pond. She is the non-dual Wisdom of all Buddhas in the form of utterly powerful action. Her incessant Buddha-activity is that of healing protection and illumination. The power of her mantra brings life-giving rain and averts life-threatening disaster, as well as maturing the highest perfect Enlightenment. Her right hand lies gently on Her right knee opened in the mudra of complete generosity, and from her palm the green light of compassion-energy streams into the universe in all the ten directions.

Her left hand is poised gracefully by Her shoulder holding, between thumb and ring finger, the stem of the blue
lotus of non-dual Wisdom which blossoms beside her left
ear, sending rays of blue light into the hearts and minds
of all sentient beings. Her body, light and clear as open
space, contains not a single atom of substance but is com-
posed purely of clear seeing and intense compassion. Her
surpassingly beautiful form is created and sustained simply from the sound of the mantra that she sings subtly
with her entire body, speech, and mind, which is none
other than the Body, Speech, and Mind of all Buddhas.
Repeating this mantra our own body, speech, and mind
become absorbed utterly in that powerful current of
transcendent sound:

OM TARE TUT TARE TURE SVAHA

Drawn forth by the sincere practice of this mantra from
the luminous green body of the Goddess Tara, the Perfection of Wisdom in Action, the Mother of all yoginis and
yogis, there flows a stream of clear light into the body
of the meditator, transforming it into Her own smiling
form, as a living channel of Her blessing-waves which
are constantly flooding the entire universe, quenching
the fires of suffering. As the bright sun gradually evap-
orates the pool of rain which reflects it, so Mother Tara
draws into Herself the whole being of the meditator who
visualizes Her form. Now there is only the Goddess Tara.

Now even the transcendent form of Tara disappears
into Her Essence, which is the clear light of absolute
Mind, the perfect union of the Bliss of action and the
Void of Wisdom. Only the pure diamond sound of the
mantra remains:

OM TARE TUT TARE TURE SVAHA

From the eternal seeds of this mantra alone, there
gradually springs forth again the entire universe with the
entrancing form of the green maiden Tara seated secretly
in the hearts of all living beings. Her powerful Presence

there heals, protects, and illumines. All beings are now perceived to be existing in perfect peace, freed from the illusion of ignorance by the inconceivable Buddha-activity of the Wisdom Mother. All beings are revealed to be the Tara herself. All forms are her form. All sounds are her sounds. The entire universe is Her mandala, and She is the supreme teacher sitting in its center.

Along with all the yoginis and yogis, her daughters and sons, we take refuge in Tara, reverently requesting from Her the initiation that intensifies practice and accelerates Enlightenment, that She may shine through our body, speech, and mind as the gift of supreme happiness to all that lives.

OM TARE TUT TARE TURE SVAHA

Clues revealing the universal characteristics of Holy Wisdom or Sophia are the references to the light within nature, to the non-dual or unified quality of that wisdom, the "blue" rays, and the invisible energy-waves of the goddess. She is invisible and yet becomes visible to those who practice her wisdom. The prayer is sheer poetry, to analyze it further seems almost sacrilegious.

In Kabbalism, the mystical tradition of Judaism, the name of Sophia is "Chokmah," and the Tree is the Tree of the Sephiroth. For the Kabbalist the Shekinah is the equivalent of Shakti energy, and the concept of wisdom hiding in sparks of light is also in that tradition. The depths and heights and embracing totality of the study of the Kabbalah are so vast that one can only hint that here, too, is a joyous pursuit in which symbolism, colors, numbers, etymology, gematria, geometry are all conjoined waiting for the student of esotericism.

The natural life has never been repressed in Judaism, and the feminine is seen as essential. The wife is the Queen of the Sabbath. What has been hardest for some women of that creed is the exclusion from intellectual participation in the study of the faith of their fathers.

I remember a dramatic stalemate on the Chi-ops trip, when the ship docked at Haifa. A group of Hasidic musicians and dancers, all men, came aboard to entertain the group. The music was lively and soon we were tapping our feet and clapping hands. However, when some of the young women in our group got up to dance themselves, the musicians abruptly put down their instruments, saying it was against their religious views to allow women to dance to their music. To this Fritjof Capra took exception, and he suggested that all the women who disagreed with this and felt the rule should be changed in the New Age should walk out, and a large contingent did just that. This was a real cultural clash of mythologies. I myself was in the restroom at that moment, and so missed having to decide whether the principle or the injunction to respect other people's customs and hospitality was more important.

In the words of the late great Rabbi Avraham Kook of Jerusalem, republished by the journal *Gnosis:*

> All things that exist draw their light from the most sublime Source. Every dimension of being, every creation is a revelation of the infinite Light. Throughout our lives these creations have appeared to us in fragmentary ways as sparks of light. But now that we grasp their true essence, we know that they are parts of a single organism, a single revelation embracing all beauty, all illumination, all truth, and all goodness...

The flood of joy flowing through this goodness lifts the soul to its Source. We behold the worlds of matter and spirit filled with splendor, knowing that they would be utterly insignificant if they stood alone, detached from their Source.

I went looking for you and found you in what we call the Polar Bear den. You were struggling with income taxes! But I handed you what I had written.

You read it and smiled at me, and then you said, "Would it be possible, do you suppose, to jot down some practical applications of all this? You know, I am convinced of the reality of this Comforter. I can even picture my own fairy godmother, though I might be more apt to say 'a little bird told me,' because that's the way I feel about my own intuition. It doesn't pay for me to read books that tell me I am asleep. Supposing I want to wake up! How would one go about playing Sophia's game? Are there any rules, any helpful instructions to make it easier?"

I went back into my library and thought about it. Outside the window I could see the snow falling gently and persistently. Perhaps there are hints for playing "Mondayschool," to Sophia's hide-and-seek. They worked for me, so at least I could share them. But I suspect that for each individual they might be just a little bit different, because each of us processes experience itself in a unique way. It would be interesting and fun to try.

Heaven is spread about upon the earth but men do not see it.
        The Gospel according to Thomas

There is another world. It is hidden in this one.
                        Anonymous

Astrology is a symbolic language of archetypal processes. It is a language Sophia speaks.

It is our own awareness which sanctifies.
                        A.O.

God has said, "There are seventy thousand veils between you and Me, but there are no veils between Me and you."
        Sheikh Muzaffer Ozak

XIII

$\mathcal{M}$ondayschool

On Iona it was almost impossible to keep from finding Sophia's wisdom in nature, but now that we were home and winter coming, we were forced to spend more hours indoors among our commonplace things—objects.

I remembered two valuable insights I owed to my coffee makers. The first pot was a double-globed, Chemex one, very like an alchemical retort. During meditation, it kept appearing to me, much to my puzzlement. So I asked why. The insight was that this was a demonstration of the very process of meditation. By turning on the heat beneath the water in the lower vessel (one's intention), the heat forced the water up into the higher vessel. There it came in contact with the "coffee," put in by a higher agent (the Divine Guest, the Self). Then, when the heat was turned off, the fresh coffee slowly descended to the lower vessel and was ready for use. The signal of readiness was a final little gluggle. This was the equivalent of the "aha!"—the little attack of insight that is Sophia's trademark. This also was an explanation why answers do not come immediately.

181

The second coffee maker, my present one, involves a paper filter. This is a different process from the former one, since the hot water is poured down from above. In the morning, I would take special pleasure in the fresh, white, virginal filter paper I put into the receptacle. It gave such a crisp start to any day. Then, one morning, it hit me. It was the "virginal" quality that stuck in my mind, and I remembered all that I had read about the extraordinary lengths to which the Church Fathers had gone, caught in their own literalism, to explain the actual technique of the Virgin Birth. Did Mary have a hymen? Did she menstruate? Did she conceive through her ear? And so forth. What the filter paper was reminding me of was the fact that every month the womb relines itself with a fresh placenta, and so the feminine is both constant and fresh at one and the same time. In a way, then, every birth is a virgin birth. The coffee tasted excellent that morning!

The psychological level of the Virgin Birth gives us another insight, of course, and since almost every avatar is said to have had a virgin birth, it would seem to point to the inner birth of what the alchemist called the *filius sapientiae*, the son of Sophia, the Divine Child, of the incarnating Self. Here the term "psychological" borders on the spiritual, and so we can be led through symbols to more profound revelations. The difference, for me at any rate, is that these matters cease to be only articles of faith or doctrine, but test out in my daily life of the commonplace. When I first read the definition that a symbol is a theophany (a revelation of God) of the Absolute in the relative, I quailed. Now I cheerfully agree. In fact, the very words trip off my tongue with glee.

To many, this may seem to be a ludicrous, if not irreverent means to approach the deeper mysteries of theology, but it is a way of showing where we can start.
My reverence is all the greater for realizing that, through
a deeper awareness, every moment of my life could be
seen to be precious and sacred. If we can find this secret
under our very noses, all about us, we can begin the slow
ascent of levels of meaning with a firm basis in the
material world. Then the "mysteries" are grounded; they
make *sense,* and we need not feel so threatened by the
mysterium tremendum. We can feel comforted by the
Paraclete (the Comforter) and experience, like children,
the joys of learning just a little more through a more
direct experience. Sophia's approach, I truly believe,
makes wisdom more accessible. It does not take the
place, in any way, of the Logos, or the masculine approach, yet it supports it. Mary-Sophia, the Virgin
within us all, holds us tenderly to her breast, a lasting
icon of Wisdom and also of love.

So perhaps Sophia wants us to appreciate the fact that
the more we dialogue with nature and with the simple
objects around us, the greater our intuition and our skill
at making connections can become in interacting also
with people, family and friends, and clients and patients
(for those of us in the helping professions). These connections can constitute a whole vocabulary with which
to communicate abstract concepts in concrete terms.
More than that, they enable one to practice what M suggested about following a twig back to its roots. It can
enable us, as well, to decode the images presented to
us in dreams, in verbal expressions, in the "as ifs" of archetypal subpersonalities which might or might not be

indwelling fragments coming from other lifetimes. As it is said in the Gospel of Philip, one of the *Nag Hammadi* documents, "Truth comes not naked but appears to us in types and images."

Sophia has also been appearing, it seems, in people's dreams. One woman client brought me a painting of a dream figure, which I have attempted to reproduce below:

The figure is feminine, holding a dove, and she is joining the Sun and the Moon. Her gown is green, and she is standing on a rock in the cleft of a mountain. One hand touches the earth, and the other holds the dove aloft. My client felt the figure to be a numinous guide within her.

Another woman client shared a remarkable dream which ended with the following image:

I am back in the hotel and have on jogging clothes. I am sitting just inside a closet—broom closet, a utility room—sitting on the floor—fanny in the closet, feet in the hall, the door open fully. The hall is filled with buckets, mops, brooms, and vacuum cleaners. A little dog goes by and partially closes the door in order to get by. He is playful and sits on my lap, and I pet him. I look up and see a very old woman. She also has on sweats and is carrying a mop and vacuum. She sits across from me on the floor. The wall she is leaning against is made up of squares of mirrors and I see many reflections. She had a hat that was so whimsical that I had to giggle. The hat was in two layers. The first layer on her head was a circle, and from that came spokes, and at the end of each spoke another smaller circle, and through each circle was a cone—each one a color of the rainbow. On top of the circle were four little columns holding up a smaller circle—again with little spokes and smaller circles, and in each one, birthday party flowers all in colors of the rainbow. She sat opposite me and opened a lunch box and started to eat. She had a wonderful twinkle in her eyes and an impish smile. Her whole being radiated love for me. I awoke laughing.

The dream came to me when I was in despair. I think of it often because it makes me feel wonderful, yet when I talk about the old woman I weep.

Here again is Sophia masquerading as the Fairy Godmother appropriately with both a touch of the absurd and the humorous. The dream concludes with strong indications that the dreamer is longing to "clean up" her act, and her Fairy Godmother appears to help her. As the woman told me her dream, her eyes filled with tears, so powerful was the affect. No robes of glory here for Sophia—dressed in "sweats," she was ready to go, crazy hat and all!

With this in mind, and with some trepidation, I heard again your request for a few suggestions to aid in eliciting or summoning up Sophia from one's unconscious. The idea came to provide a little manual, a *vademecum*, for playing Sophia's game. Accordingly, I have divided this little manual into three parts.

HOW TO PLAY SOPHIA'S HIDE-AND-SEEK

STAGE ONE

Materials: A commonplace book (a personal notebook, preferably not looseleaf) and an available pen or pencil. Into this book go the odd thoughts and/or quotations that really elicit an "aha!" Sacrifice any sense of order or category, but keep an alphabetical index at the end for handy reference.

Location: your own *temenos.*
If possible, one small space or corner in your home or apartment where you can lead your symbolic life. Light a candle, and after meditating, say a prayer asking for insight, but expect nothing to happen *at that moment.* (It probably won't. Attacks of insight usually strike at the most inconvenient time possible. That's part of the fun. The trick is to see how fast you can catch and fix the insight on a piece of paper. In the beginning you will find obscure notes and gems of wisdom in your pocket, purse, or on napkins, backs of envelopes, etc. Hang on to them! Then, add them to your commonplace book.)

In the meantime, just for practice, begin with contemplating the nature of fire, the need for candles.

—How are we like them?

—How many could you light from this one?

—What sayings go with a candle? (Example: "Better to light one candle than curse the darkness?")

—Using your imagination, place ten candles in different lanterns. How could they teach you to love even those you don't like?

—Jot down any sayings, stories, parables, myths, or prayers connected to fire, to light, or to the Sun that you know. Add these to them.

(Here's one to the Sun from the Sanskrit: *"You, who are the source of all power, whose rays illuminate the whole world, illuminate also my heart so that it, too, can do your work."*)

—Meditate on the meaning of "enlightenment."

—Contemplate how different the element of fire is from those of earth, air, and water.

—How do these physically interact?

—What could be their symbolic counterparts in you?

In subsequent days, place a bowl of water in the room, then a plant potted in earth, and finally, open a window to let the air circulate. Become aware of all the elements. Continue asking questions, setting down insights, looking for commonplace phrases of speech that pertain to these four elements. Branch out and experiment on your own.

Next, extend your meditations to the symbolism of the seven colors of the rainbow, or the meaning of a simple box, or a zipper, or a corkscrew, etc. Very soon you can use your meditation for its original purpose of worship and concentration, but the habit of expectant attention

in your everyday life will have been set. You will never
be bored again!

Very often Sophia communicates through "simulacra." This is a spontaneous phenomenon which occurs
when you look at one thing and see another, a face, a
figure, etc. It is at the basis not only of the famous psychological Rorschach Test, but also the "reading" of tea
leaves or what have you. Simulacra come easily to most
children and poets. Give them more space in your thinking.

STAGE TWO

Materials: Skeat's *Etymological Dictionary*

A dictionary of symbols (see Bibliography; there are
several)

Man and his Symbols by Carl Gustav Jung

any books on mythology—classical, Celtic,
Indian...

fairy tales: Grimm's, Andrew Lang's collections

any book on elementary astrology or my own
Jungian Symbolism in Astrology, which is geared
to this way of thinking

books on Sacred Geometry

Suggestions: Begin to look for the *process* hidden in any
thing, and then extend it symbolically through various
levels until you reach its archetypal or psychological
meaning.

Example: *A CUP*

Object: any cup

Process: containing, passively receiving, actively pouring; a feminine process (why?)

Body: breasts, stomach, womb

Symbolic: chalice, winner's cup, St. John the Divine Tarot suit, Hearts

Mythic: Bran's cauldron, Holy Grail, Mother Goddess as container of all life, Mother Earth, Sophia, et al.

Astrological: Moon (why?)

Psychological/Spiritual: soul, psyche as vessel of consciousness and unconsciousness, ego (ideally)

Sophia, as receiving experience and transforming facts into knowledge; knowledge applied into experience; experience into wisdom through intuition!

N.B. This is a minute sampling of what further extensions a dictionary of symbols might provide. However, it is highly preferable to allow your own intuition to provide the associations. In that way the process becomes *meaningful to you.* Soon, your own unconscious will respond actively in dreams and synchronicities. For instance, you will be able to find a galaxy as you stir the cream into your own coffee cup. (Its spiral follows the same mathematics as a spiral nebula or water flushing down a drain or even the cowlick on a baby's head!)

STAGE THREE

Materials: The Holy Bible,
    the Sacred Texts of other religions:
    The Bhagavad Gita

The Upanishads
The *Gospel of Ramakrishna*
The *I Ching* (Richard Wilhelm trans.)
American Indian and/or African texts
Zen texts

For appreciation: Joseph Campbell's *The Masks of God*
Books on the goddesses (there are many)
Browse in libraries and the paperback sections of bookstores. *Use* your paperbacks! Underline.

Progress from things to contemplating archetypal activities (verbs). This is the essence of alchemy.

Examples: Building and tearing down a scaffold.

Knitting: we learn best by "knitting" new knowledge into the fabric of what we already know. Then it is secured.

Embroidery: grounding one stitch at a time in the fabric. Backstitch!

Weaving, spinning, cooking.

Hammering, sawing, joining, turning, churning

Farming, herding (two great historical divisions resulting in two major approaches to religion!)

The mysteries of relationships, the nature of the different kinds of love

Anatomy, the functions of each organ or system and what they contribute to the whole body. Find the psychological counterpart in terms of process. Here astrology comes in.

Computer processes!

I hesitate to suggest more, since the whole point is to start with the simplest and work on up through the variations on any theme. Anything around the house, the office, or the garden will do for Sophia to reveal her various elementary processes that link up and make connections from the simplest (the ridiculous, if you will) to the most sublime, the deepest, and most holy mysteries of life itself. The essential rule of Sophia's game is to look through whatever you happen to be doing and find the psychological or spiritual implication or connections that can lead you not only to a deeper understanding of yourself, but to the decoding of nature and even religious ritual and liturgy, the symbolic meaningfulness of which has very often been lost, and is very rarely taught.

For instance, some of the alchemical verbs hide in our kitchens, as well as our psyches. They are:

calcinatio—burning, sometimes down to ashes

solutio—dissolving, as salt in water

coagulatio—coagulating, as in vanilla pudding or bread

mortificatio—the death of one state of food before becoming another. Raw into cooked.

separatio—chopping, slicing, carving, dismembering, separating ingredients

sublimating—as with the duck (see p. 132) or the meal prepared with such love, it becomes a feast that nourishes the very soul. Holy Communion.

coniunctio—Sophia's magical *omnia coniungo*, the process of uniting the ingredients, the four elements hidden within the food, and hiding in the Grace that both precedes and follows after such a meal. The love hidden in the food, in its preparation, and in its sharing.

Even in this most elementary description, everything is carried on in the vessels (pots) of the cook, in the greater container of the kitchen, in the yet greater container of the house or home, and on and on, so that symbolically—by extension—the entire opus or Work is performed, daily, all over the world. Yet mostly we remain unconscious of the fact that even in this simplest fulfilling of our daily needs we are partaking of the holiest mysteries of the sacred within the commonplace of our own kitchen. Once these operations become more conscious, we can be ready to see these same alchemical operations being acted out in the very vessel of our own psyches, and then we are ready for Jung and Edinger's studies of alchemy as stages in the individuation process.

There is a Latin proverb: *Multum in parvo.* It suggests that the great is to be found in the little. The macrocosm hidden in the microcosm. The "As above, so below," or as without, so within.

When I finished writing these words, I wanted you to read them. I found you in the kitchen making lunch so that I could work. Without thinking, we gave each other a hug of gratitude. Then you turned to stir the soup and I heard you laugh.

"Do you know what I think?" you said. "That dove can only be released from the stone through love."

CELTIC PRAYER

God bless to me the new day,
Never vouchsafed to me before;
It is to bless Thine own presence
Thou hast given me this time, O God.

Bless thou to me mine eye
May mine eye bless all it sees;
I will bless my neighbour,
May my neighbour bless me.

God, give me a clean heart,
Let me not from the sight of Thine eye;
Bless to me my children and my spouse,
And bless to me my means and my cattle.
                    From the Carmina Gadelica

Bibliography

Albertson, Charles, ed. 1932. *Lyra mystica: An anthology of mystical verse.* New York: Macmillan.

Aquinas, Thomas. 1966. *Aurora consurgens.* Marie-Louise von Franz, ed. New York: Pantheon.

Ardalan, Nader, and Laleh Bakhtiar. 1979. *The sense of unity: The Sufi tradition in Persian architecture.* Publications of the Center for Middle Eastern Studies. Chicago: University of Chicago Press.

Augustine, Saint. 1943. *Confessions.* New York: Sheed and Ward.

Avalon, Arthur (Sir John Woodroffe). 1978. *Shakti and Shakta.* New York: Dover Publications, Inc.

Bamford, Christopher, and William Parker Marsh. 1987. *Celtic Christianity: Ecology and holiness.* West Stockbridge, MA: Inner Traditions/Lindisfarne Press.

Bauer, Wolfgang, et al., eds. 1980. *Lexicon der symbole.* Wiesbaden: Fourier Verlag.

Bayley, Harold. 1952. *The lost language of symbolism.* 2 vols. London: Williams and Norgate.

The book of common prayer. 1892. Oxford: Oxford University Press.

Boulgakov, Pero Serge. 1983. *La sagesse de Dieu: résumé de sophiologie.* Constantin Andronikov, tr. Lausanne: L'Age d'Homme.

Bulfinch, Thomas. 1970. *Bulfinch's mythology.* 2nd rev. ed. New York: Harper Junior Books.

Campbell, Joseph. 1959. *The masks of god, vol. I: Primitive mythology.* New York: Viking.

————. 1962. *The masks of god, vol. II: Oriental mythology.* New York: Viking.

————. 1964. *The masks of god, vol. III: Occidental mythology.* New York: Viking.

————. 1968. *The masks of god, vol. IV: Creative mythology.* New York: Viking.

————. 1974. *The mythic image.* Bollingen Series C. Princeton: Princeton University Press.

Carmichael, Alexander. 1986. *The new moon of the seasons: Prayers from the highlands and islands.* Worcester, England: Billing and Sons, Ltd.

Carter, Robert. 1988. *The Tao and Mother Goose.* Wheaton, IL: Theosophical Publishing House, Quest Books.

Cassirer, Ernst. 1971. *The philosophy of symbolic forms: Mythical thought.* 2 vols. New Haven: Yale University Press.

Chevalier, Jean, and Alain Gheerbrant, eds. 1973. *Dictionnaire des symboles.* Paris: Séghers.

Conze, Edward, et al., eds. 1964. *Buddhist texts through the ages.* New York: Harper and Row.

Corbin, Henry. 1977. *Spiritual body and celestial earth: From Mazdean Iran to Shi'ite Iran.* Princeton: Princeton University Press.

De Vries, Ad. 1981. *Dictionary of symbols and imagery.* Amsterdam: North Holland Publishing Co.

De Waal, Esther. 1985. *God under my roof.* Fairacres Oxford: SLG.

Donnell, Ernest W.M. 1954. *The beguines and beghards.* New Brunswick, NJ: Rutgers University Press.

Edinger, Edward F. 1972. *Ego and archetype: Individuation and the religious function of the psyche.* New York: G.P. Putnam and Sons.

————. 1985. *The anatomy of the psyche.* La Salle, IL: Open Court.

Eliade, Mircea. 1960. *Myths, dreams, and mysteries: The encounter between contemporary faiths and archaic realities.* Philip Mairet, tr. New York: Harper and Row.

————. 1968. *Myth and reality.* Willard R. Trask, tr. New York: Harper and Row.

————. 1985. *A History of religious ideas.* Willard R. Trask, Jr. 3 vols. Chicago: The University of Chicago Press.

Finlay, Ian. 1979. *Columba*. London: Victor Gollancz, Ltd.

Fox, Matthew. 1980. *Breakthrough: Meister Eckhart's creation spirituality in new translation*. Garden City, NY: Doubleday.

_____. 1983. *Meditations with Meister Eckhart*. Santa Fe, NM: Sun Bear and Co.

Fremantle, Anne. 1971. *Woman's Way to God*. New York: St. Martin's Press.

Gaskell, G.A. 1960. *Dictionary of all scriptures and myths*. New York: Julian Press, Inc.

Grimm, Jacob, and Wilhelm Grimm. 1986. *Grimm's Fairy Tales*. New York: Western Publications, Golden Press.

Herder lexikon: Germanische und Keltische mythologie. 1980. Freiburg: Herder Verlag.

Hoagland, Kathleen, ed. 1962. *1000 years of Irish poetry*. New York: Grosset and Dunlap.

The Holy Bible: King James version. 1928. Oxford: Oxford University Press.

Howell, Alice O. 1987. *Jungian symbolism in astrology: Letters from an astrologer*. Wheaton, IL: The Theosophical Publishing House, Quest Books.

Hughes, Gerard W. 1984. *God of surprises*. London: Dartman, Longman and Todd, Ltd.

Jobes, Gertrude. *Dictionary of mythology, folklore, and symbols*. New York: The Scarecrow Press, Inc.

Jonas, Hans. 1963. *The gnostic religion: The message of the alien god and the beginnings of Christianity*. Boston: Beacon Press.

Jung, Carl Gustav. 1957-1979. *The collected works*. R.F.C. Hull, tr. Bollingen Series, 20 vols. Princeton: Princeton University Press.

Kingsford, Anna Bonus. 1937. *Clothed with the sun: Being the book of the illuminations*. London: John M. Watkins.

Kook, Rav Abraham. 1986-7. A thirst for the living God. Burt Jacobson, tr. *Gnosis 3: A Journal of the Western Inner Traditions*. Fall/Winter. San Francisco: Lumen Foundations.

Krishna, Gopi. 1967. *Kundalini: the evolutionary energy in man*. Boulder, CO: Shambhala Press.

Kuskin, Karla. 1987. *Something's sleeping in the hall.* New York: Harper and Row.

Leach, Maria, ed. 1949. *Dictionary of folklore, mythology, and legend.* New York: Funk and Wagnalls.

Luke, Helen M. 1961. *Women, earth, and spirit: The feminine in symbol and myth.* New York: The Crossroad Publishing Company.

Macleod, Fiona. 1985. *Iona.* Edinburgh: The Floris Press.

McGlashan, Alan. 1967. *The savage and beautiful country.* Boston: Houghton and Mifflin.

Merry, Eleanor C. 1969. *The flaming door.* East Grinstead, England: New Knowledge Books.

Mukerjee, Ajit, and Madhu Khanna. 1977. *The tantric way: Art, science, ritual.* Boston: New York Graphic Society.

Nelli, René. Undated. Dictionnaire des héresies méridionales. France: privately printed.

Neumann, Erich. 1974. *The great mother: An analysis of the archetype.* Princeton: Princeton University Press.

O'Driscoll, Herbert. 1986. *A doorway in time.* New York: Harper and Row.

O'Driscoll, Robert O., ed. 1981. *The Celtic consciousness.* Edinburgh: Canongate Publishing House.

Paracelsus. 1969. *Selected writings.* Jolande Jacobi, ed. Bollingen Series XXVIII. Princeton: Princeton University Press.

Paterson, John L. Undated. *Iona: A celebration.* London: John Murray, Ltd.

Petroff, Elizabeth Avilda. 1986. *Medieval women's visionary literature.* New York: Oxford University Press.

Robinson, James M., gen. ed. 1977. *The Nag Hammadi library in English.* New York: Harper and Row.

Runion, Garth E. 1972. *The golden section and related curiosa.* Glenview, IL: Scott, Foresman and Co.

Schaupp, Joan. 1975. *Woman: Image of the Holy Spirit.* Denville, NJ: Dimension Books.

Schmidt, K. O. 1975. *The message of the Grail.* Lakemont, GA: CSA Press.

Schwaller de Lubicz, R.A. 1982. *Nature word: verbe nature.* Deborah Lawlor, tr. West Stockbridge, MA: Lindisfarne Press.

Skeat, Walter W. 1882. *An etymological dictionary of the English language*. Oxford: Clarendon Press.

Slesinski, Robert. 1984. *Pavel Florensky: A metaphysics of love*. Crestwood, NY: St. Vladimir's Seminary Press.

Swire, Otta. 1964. *The Inner Hebrides and their legends*. London: Collins.

Thomas, Saint. 1983. *The gospel according to Thomas*. Sacred Texts Series. Santa Barbara, CA: Concord Grove Press.

Towill, Edwin Sprott. Undated. *The saints of Scotland*. Edinburgh: The Saint Andrew Press.

Ulanov, Ann Belford. 1971. *The feminine in Jungian psychology and Christian theology*. Evanston, IL: Northwestern University Press.

Underhill, Evelyn. 1960. *Mysticism*. New York: Meridian Books.

Von Franz, Marie-Louise. 1972. *The feminine in fairy tales*. Zurich: Spring Publications.

Von Nettesheim, Heinrich Cornelius Agrippa. 1982. *Die magischen werke*. Wiesbaden: Fourir Verlag, G.m.b.H.

Walker, Barbara G. 1083. *The woman's encyclopedia of myths and secrets*. New York: Harper and Row.

Weil, Simone. 1956. *The notebooks of Simone Weil*. London: Routledge and Kegan Paul.

Whitmont, Edward C. 1980. *The return of the goddess*. New York: Crossroads.

QUEST BOOKS
are published by
The Theosophical Society in America,
Wheaton, Illinois 60189-0270,
a branch of a world organization
dedicated to the promotion of brotherhood and
the encouragement of the study of religion,
philosophy, and science, to the end that man may
better understand himself and his place in
the universe. The Society stands for complete
freedom of individual search and belief.
In the Classics Series well-known
theosophical works are made
available in popular editions.